Th
Beav

SPORTING RULES

Compiled by Lea Clarke

Illustrated by Bob Harvey

Beaver Books

First published in 1980 by
The Hamlyn Publishing Group Limited
London · New York · Sydney · Toronto
Astronaut House, Feltham, Middlesex, England

ISBN 0 600 38369 5

Filmset, printed and bound in Great Britain
by Hazell Watson & Viney Limited
Aylesbury, Bucks
Set in Univers

Contents

Introduction

Official books of rules are formidable documents, full of phrases such as ' "Controlling Body" (which means the body having immediate control of the conditions under which a match is played) or 'Subject to the exception of Law F, 10, the ball shall be awarded at the point where it is declared out of bounds by the Referee to the nearest player of the team opposing that of the player who last touched it.'

Rules are worded in this way because they have to cover all the unexpected incidents that may happen during play. Yet most people want just a simple list of the basic rules so that they can understand quickly how to play a game correctly, or follow what is happening when they watch a sport live or on television. That is what this book sets out to do.

So you will not find every detailed rule here, but I have tried to give you enough information to enable you to enjoy the games you play and watch. Where there are different rules for amateurs and professionals, I have given only the amateur rules.

Have fun!

L.C.

Note on Metrication

Most sports are changing over to metric units, but imperial units are still sometimes used by players and officials.

In this book we have given the official metric measurements where possible, but used traditional terms, such as 'ten yard line', where these are still in common use.

ACKNOWLEDGEMENTS

I am indebted to the following organisations for their help in compiling this book:

Grand National Archery Society
Amateur Athletic Association
Badminton Association of England
Baseball Association of Great Britain
English Basketball Association
Billiards and Snooker Control Council
British Bobsleigh Association
English Bowling Association
Amateur Boxing Association
Marylebone Cricket Club
The Croquet Association
British Cycling Federation
British Darts Organisation
Amateur Fencing Association
Canadian High Commission
Football Association
Rugby Football Union
Royal and Ancient Golf Club of St. Andrews, Fife
British Amateur Gymnastics Association
International Hockey Rules Board
British Ice Hockey Association
National Skating Association of Great Britain
British Judo Association
Martial Arts Commission
English Lacrosse Union
Lawn Tennis Association
Auto-Cycle Union
British Motor Sports Council
All England Netball Association
British Orienteering Federation
National Rounders Association
Camanachd Association
British Horse Society
National Ski Federation of Great Britain
British Tenpin Bowling Association
Squash Rackets Association
International Table Tennis Federation
English Volleyball Association
British Amateur Wrestling Association
Norman S. Barrett, sports consultant

ARCHERY

Shooting with a bow and arrows needs a good eye and steady hands. It is a skill that was very important when people had to hunt game for food, and when bows and arrows were important weapons of war. These days archers aim at straw targets, and the nearer they get to the centre of the target the more points they score. There are two basic kinds of archery, target and field. There are special rules for juniors – archers under 18 year of age – but these mainly relate to the kinds of rounds (number of shots) that juniors shoot, and the national competition rules.

In target archery you shoot at the butts, targets mounted on straw mats. A number of targets are lined up side by side. Each target is marked with a series of rings, coloured (from the centre outwards) gold, red, blue, black and white. You score 9 points for a hit in the gold, 7 for red, 5 for blue, 3 for black and 1 for white. If your arrow touches two adjoining colours you score the value of the higher colour. You may use only an approved kind of bow, and it can be fitted with not more than four stabilisers – weighted arms which help you to keep the bow steady.

A round is the number of shots you are allowed in a contest. There are many rounds, each with their own numbers of arrows. In the York Round, one of the most famous, you shoot 72 arrows at 100 yards, 48 arrows at 80 yards, and 24 arrows at 60 yards. Juniors may shoot adult rounds, but they also have their own rounds, the Bristol Rounds, numbered I to IV. Girls under 13 and boys under 12 enter for the Bristol IV, girls under 16 and boys under 14 for Bristol III, girls under 18 and boys under 16 for Bristol II, and boys under 18 for Bristol I. You can enter a competition for people older than yourself,

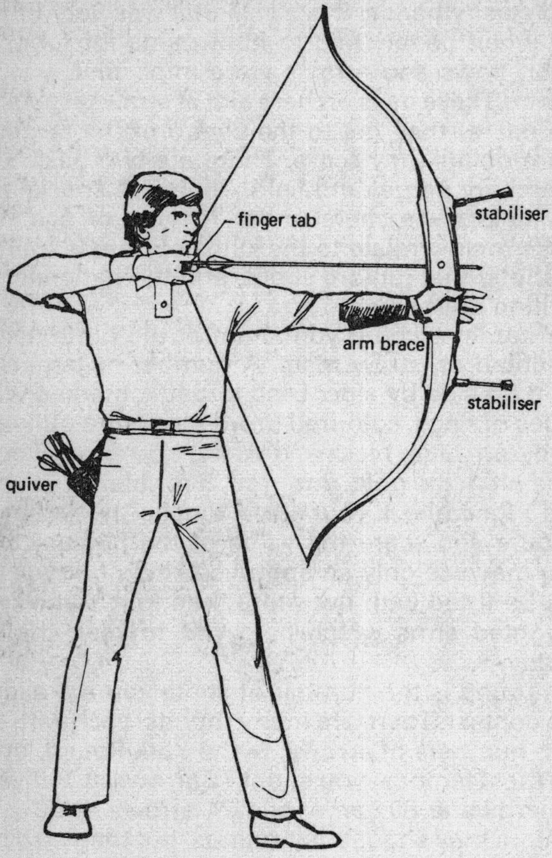
finger tab
stabiliser
arm brace
stabiliser
quiver

but not one for younger people. The distances for Bristol IV are shorter than for Bristol III, and so on.

During a round you shoot three arrows at a time; they are checked and removed and the score added up. You must shoot standing up, unless you are disabled.

In field archery, 14 targets are set out along a course in woodland or open ground. The targets are black and white, and consist of an inner spot, an inner ring, and an outer ring. These targets are used for the field round and the hunter's round. For the forester's and big game rounds, the targets are of animal or bird design, with the rings marked on them. The 14 targets are of four different sizes. You shoot four arrows at each target; the value of the arrows varies according to the round.

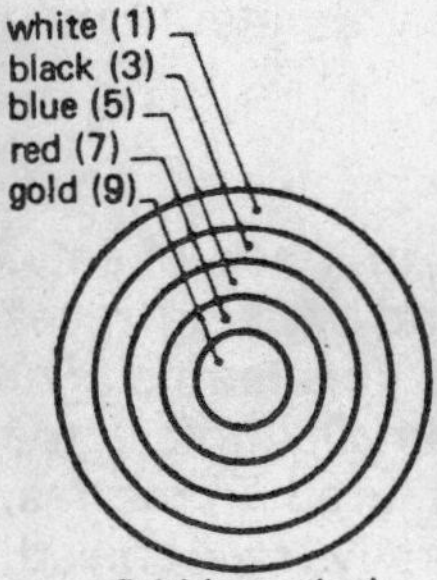

British standard

Field round

Hunter's round

ATHLETICS

Athletics is really a group of sports in which you can compete in a series of events. The sports are divided into two groups: track events, in which you race along a track over various distances; and field events, in which you jump or throw various objects. From these two groupings comes the name by which athletics is known in the United States, track and field. There are more than 50 different events for men and women, and there are some special rules for younger boys and girls.

People have been taking part in athletics contests for thousands of years. In 776 B.C. the first Olympic Games were held at Olympia in western Greece. The games were abolished in A.D. 394, but revived as an international contest in 1896. The Olympics are held every four years, and only amateurs may compete in them.

Track Events

There are five kinds of races in track events: running, hurdles, steeplechase and walking races for individuals, and relay races for teams. For international events, such as the Olympics, the distances of the races are measured in metres, though the mile event is generally recognised. Countries still using customary measurements also run events over distances measured in yards.

Races are run mostly on oval tracks, marked out into six or eight lanes. Because the outer track is longer than the inner track, competitors have staggered starts – that is, they start at different distances along the track so that they all have exactly the same distance to run. If you are running in any race under 800 metres you stay in the same lane all the way. For the 800 metres race you begin in a lane, then after a certain distance you can 'break', that is change lanes. In races over 800 metres there are no lanes.

For races under 800 metres runners use starting blocks to give them a greater grip on the track for starting. For races up to 440 yards (400 metres) the starter gives the commands 'On your marks', at which you take up your position, and 'Set', at which you stay abolutely still. He then fires a starting pistol. For longer races the command 'Set' is omitted. The winner of a race is the competitor whose chest crosses the finishing line first (arms, legs and head do not count). The finish is generally marked by a tape.

When running, you must not jostle or obstruct any other competitor, and you must not have any help from outside the track – but in races over 16 kilometres (10 miles) you may be handed refreshments.

Track relay events are run between teams of four runners. Each of the four runs one lap or one stage of the race. In a relay event you carry a baton in your hand. At the end of each stage of the race there is a hand-over zone 20 metres (22 yards) long. In this stretch your successor must take hold of the baton. You then drop out and your team-mate carries on. You must complete the hand-over within the marked zone or the team is disqualified.

In a hurdles race you have to clear a series of obstacles called hurdles, which are designed to fall over fairly easily if touched. There are usually 10 hurdles to clear in each race, and you must jump over them all. You must not swing a leg round a hurdle, or deliberately knock it over with your hand or foot. Women jump over lower hurdles than men, and younger competitors use lower hurdles still. Distances vary; in the Olympics they are 110 metres and 400 metres for men, and 100 metres for women.

Walking races are events usually for men. In a

An athletics stadium

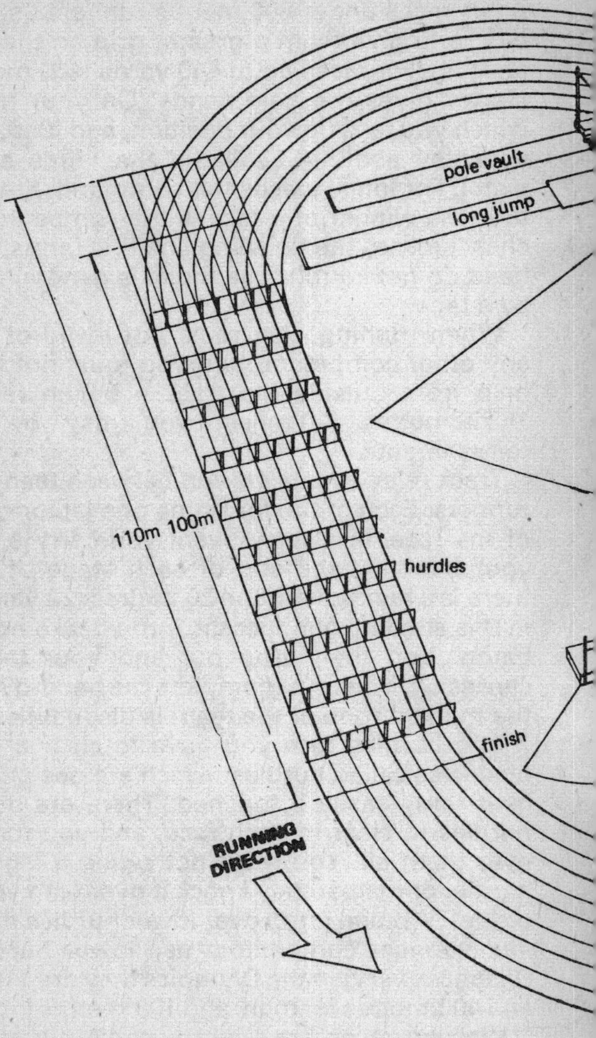

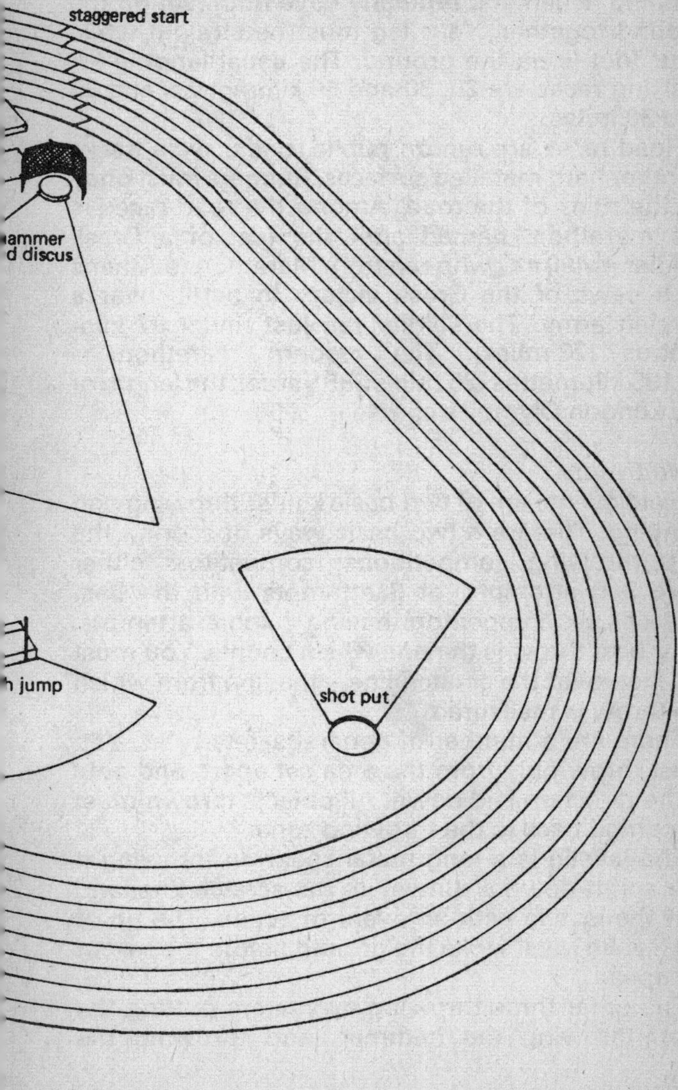
staggered start
ammer
d discus
h jump
shot put

walking race, your front foot must touch the ground before your rear foot leaves it – as distinct from running, when you regularly have both feet off the ground together. Your leg must be straight while your foot is on the ground. The usual lengths for walking races are 20, 30 and 50 kilometres, and 20 and 30 miles.

Road races are run on public roads, cycle tracks or other hard metalled surfaces. Runners must obey all the rules of the road. Among the road races is the marathon, named after the feat of a Greek soldier in 490 B.C., who ran from Marathon to Athens with news of the Greek victory in battle over a Persian army. The soldier ran just under 37 kilometres (23 miles). The modern marathon is 42·195 kilometres (26 miles 385 yards), the length of the London Olympics course in 1908.

Field Events

Field events are of two basic kinds: throwing and jumping. There are two basic ways of scoring the four throwing competitions: competitors either have 3–6 attempts, or 3 attempts with the best three or six competitors having 3 more attempts. Your best throw is the one which counts. You must not step over the scratch line – the line from which the throw is measured.

There are a number of general safety rules. You must throw only from the area set apart, and only in the direction laid down. All objects thrown must be carried back to the throwing zone.

The javelin is a long metal spear. In throwing it you sprint down a runway to the scratch line, and hurl the javelin with an overarm action. The tip of the javelin must strike the ground before the rest of the spear.

The other three throwing events are putting the shot, throwing the hammer, and throwing the discus. The shot is a solid metal ball. Men put a shot weighing 7·26 kilogrammes (16 pounds); women one weighing 4 kilogrammes (8 pounds 13 ounces). To put the shot (that is, throw it), you stand inside a circle 2·135 metres (7 feet) in diameter, which has a stop board for your feet in the direction of the throw. Your feet may make contact with the inside of the stop board, but you must not step on it, or outside the ring. You hold the shot in one hand close to your chin, and put it with a pushing action.

The discus is a flying-saucer-shaped disc with a metal rim. You hold it in one hand, spin round and release it with a sideways motion. Like the shot put, the discus is thrown from within a circle, but without the stop board. The circle is surrounded on three sides by a cage. This is for safety reasons – otherwise if a competitor let go too soon the discus could fly off in the wrong direction and hit somebody.

The hammer is also thrown from inside a cage. In ancient times the hammer used was a sledgehammer or a two-handed blacksmith's hammer. Today it is a heavy metal ball on the end of a steel wire. At the other end of the wire there is a D-shaped handle. You hold the hammer in both hands, whirl round and round within the circle, and then let the hammer go.

There are four kinds of jumping events: high jump, triple jump, long jump and pole vault.

In the high jump and the pole vault, you try to clear a crossbar supported on two metal uprights. The contest begins with the bar at a comparatively low position. The bar is raised at the end of each round. You are allowed three tries to clear the bar at each height. If you fail on all three you are eliminated. The contest goes on until all competitors but one are eliminated. You can choose to miss some of the heights, jumping only those you wish to. If you fail on two jumps at a particular height you can forego your third attempt, and re-enter at a greater height. The winner can go on jumping at greater heights than his best if he wishes to set a record. To make a clean jump in the high jump you must take off on one foot only, and you must not knock the bar down. In the pole vault you use a long, glass-fibre pole to help you gain height. You run up with the pole, put one end into a wooden or metal box provided, and spring with it. Again, you must not dislodge the bar. You can take as long a run-up as you like for the pole vault.

In the long jump and triple jump you try to jump as far forward as possible. If there are not many competitors each may be allowed 3–6 attempts; with more competitors each is allowed 3 attempts, and the three to six best have three more chances. You can take as long a run-up as you like. You take off from a board the leading edge of which marks the scratch line, from which the jumps are measured. If you take off earlier your attempt is valid, but the measurement is still made from the scratch line. You land in a bed of sand, and your distance is the nearest mark you make in the sand to the scratch line.

The triple jump is really three jumps in one, formerly called the hop, step and jump. In the hop, you take off one foot during the run up, and land on the same foot. You then take off again for the step, in which you land on the other foot, and at once take off for the third time, landing as in the long jump. You must not touch the ground with your non-jumping leg in the hop and step.

The tug-of-war is also reckoned as a branch of athletics, and it used to form part of the Olympic Games. Teams must be equal in numbers, with not more than 8 people in each team. The rope is at least 32 metres (35 yards) long. A coloured tape is tied on the rope in the middle, and the tug starts with this tape over a centre line between the two teams. There are two other lines on either side of the centre line, 2 metres (6 feet 6¾ inches) from it. The team which pulls its opponents over its own side line wins.

Another branch of athletics is cross-country running, which is very popular in some schools. In such races you run over fields, up hills and through woods. There is no set distance or type of course.

Three Olympic Games events are based on athletics. The decathlon is for men, and consists of ten events – the name 'decathlon' comes from the Greek word for ten. They are spread over two days. Each competitor has to take part in all events, and wins points according to the standard of performance. The competitor with the highest points total wins. The events are: 100 metres; long jump; shot put; high jump; 400 metres; 110 metres hurdles; throwing the discus; pole vault; throwing the javelin; and 1500 metres.

Women have a similar event called a pentathlon (from the Greek word for five). The events in it are the 100 metres hurdles; shot put; high jump; long jump; and 800 metres.

The modern pentathlon is a contest involving five very different kinds of sports: riding a strange horse; fencing; pistol-shooting; swimming; and cross-country running. Teams of three are entered by countries taking part.

BADMINTON

Badminton is derived from the ancient game of battledore and shuttlecock, which has been played in Europe for around 600 years, and in Asia for more than 2000. The modern game was first played in 1873 at Badminton, an English country estate in Gloucestershire – and that was how it got its name. It is now played in fifty countries, and it is the most popular sport in Denmark, Indonesia, Malaysia and Thailand. Although there are standard sizes for a badminton court (13·4 metres×6 metres; 44 feet×20 feet), you can easily play it on a good-sized lawn.

The badminton court is marked out as shown in the diagram. The side alleys are used only in doubles play, like the side alleys of a tennis court. The net is suspended so that its top is 1·5 metres (5 feet) above the ground. To play, you use a very light racket, with which you hit the shuttlecock, a

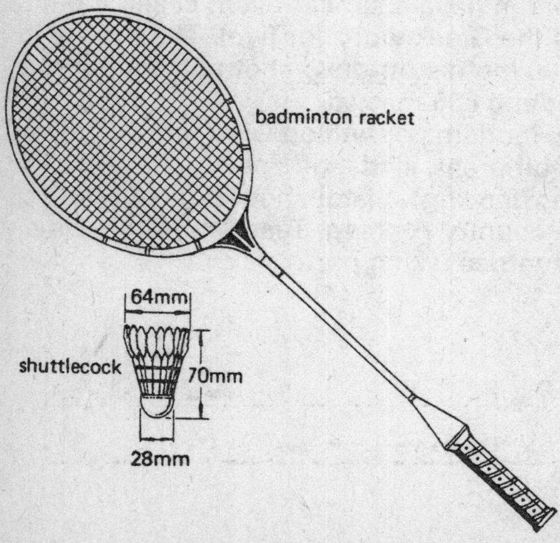

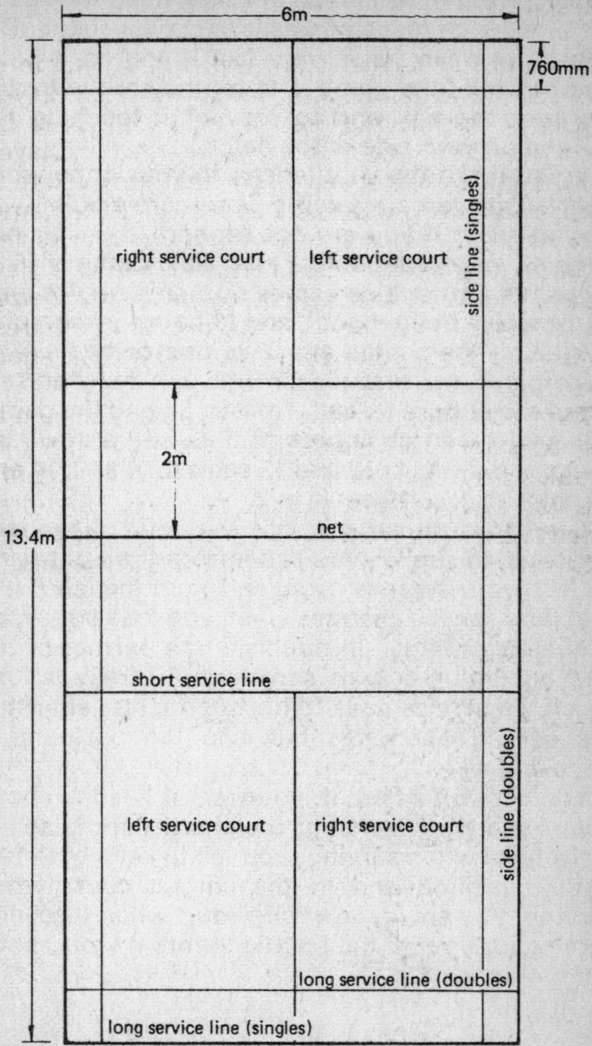
6m
760mm
right service court
left service court
side line (singles)
2m
13.4m
net
short service line
left service court
right service court
side line (doubles)
long service line (doubles)
long service line (singles)

cone-shaped object made of a cork head with up to 16 feathers, or made of plastic of similar shape. The shuttlecock can travel very fast if you hit it hard. The object of the game is to hit the shuttle to and fro over the net, and to prevent it touching the ground on your side of the net.

If you make the shuttle land in your opponent's court while you are serving, you score a point (you do not score if you are not serving). Two players (singles) or four (doubles) may play. Game is 15 or 21 points for doubles games or men's singles (you agree which beforehand), and 11 points in women's singles. If the scores are level one or two points from game the first player who has reached that score can choose to 'set' – that is, extend the game. The score then goes back to 0–0, and a new 'set' target is played. At 13 and 19 set is to 5; at 9, 14 and 20 set is to 3; at 10 set is to 2.

Serving is underhand into the court diagonally opposite. In singles you serve from the right-hand court if your score is even, and from the left if it is odd. The service changes when you lose a rally, an exchange of shots. In doubles, one partner of the pair beginning service serves until a rally is lost, when the service goes to his opponents; after that the service alternates between the partners of opposing sides.

You commit a fault if: your racket head is above your hand when serving; the shuttlecock is above waist level when serving; you fail to keep both feet on the ground and in the correct court when serving; you are in the wrong court when receiving service; or you hit the shuttle before it crosses the net to your side.

BASEBALL

Baseball is the most popular bat and ball game in North America. It is played by two nine-man teams, which take it in turns to bat. Each team tries to score more runs than the other.

The field is shown in the diagram. The infield is a square, often called 'the diamond', with sides 27·4 metres (90 feet) long. There is a base at each corner. Home plate, or base, where the batter stands, is a white rubber mat. White canvas bags mark the other bases.

The outfield extends beyond the infield on the two sides furthest from the home plate, and its size can vary. The area behind the other two sides of the infield is called foul territory.

The pitcher, who throws the ball, stands on a mound in the centre of the diamond. See the diagram for the positions of the other fielders.

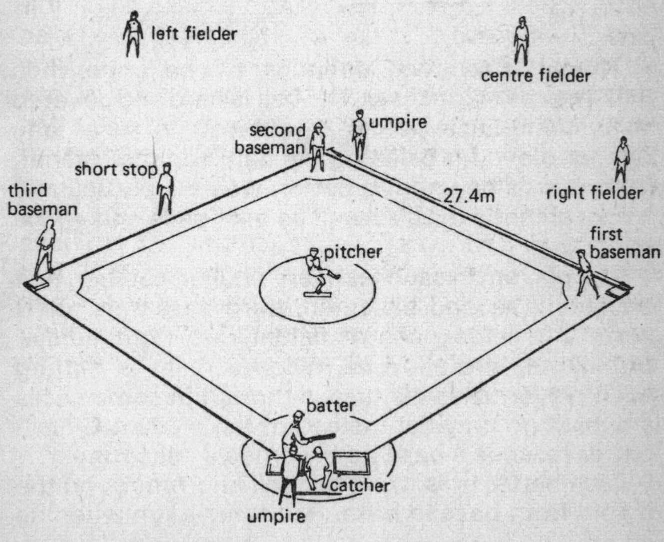

The bat is rounded, and must not be longer than 1·07 metres (42 inches). The ball is hard and covered in leather. Each fielder is allowed to wear one leather glove for catching the ball, and the catcher, who stands behind the batter, wears a particularly thick catcher's mitt, as well as shin pads and a face mask.

The players in each team are pitcher, catcher, first baseman, second baseman, third baseman, short stop, left fielder, centre fielder and right fielder. Substitutes are allowed. When a team is batting each player takes his turn, although in some cases a substitute may bat instead of the pitcher. Once a batter reaches a base he becomes a base runner.

Each batter tries to hit the ball and run round the infield from base to base. He scores a run when he reaches the home base, and a home run if he hits the ball and runs all the way round the infield to home base in one turn. The maximum possible runs that can be made at one time is four – that is when a batter scores a home run and there are already runners at first, second and third bases who also manage to reach home plate.

The batter does not have to hit the ball to go to first base. He can do so if the pitcher throws four balls outside the strike zone. Once he has reached first base he can try to steal a base, that is, sneak to the next base when an opportunity comes his way, but as only one runner may be on a base, this means that the runners before him are forced to move on to their next base, whether or not it is safe to do so.

A batter is out if a fielder catches a hit ball before it touches the ground (a fly out); if a fielder retrieves the ball and reaches the runner's base or tags him with it; and if the batter makes three strikes during his turn. He makes a strike if he swings the bat at a pitch and misses it or does not swing his bat at a pitch that the umpire declares was in the strike zone. He makes a foul strike if he hits or bunts (taps) the ball into a foul territory or if the catcher catches the ball off the bat (a foul tip).

A baseball game lasts nine innings. In an innings all the players from each team have one turn at bat until three players are out, the home team batting first.

BASKETBALL

Basketball was invented in the United States in 1891. It is now one of the most popular sports in the world, and there are more than 140,000,000 registered players. It is played by men and women of all ages, and attracts great numbers of spectators. The rules given here are based on the international amateur rules.

The court is a flat, hard (not grass) surface, 26×14 metres (85×46 feet), marked as shown in the diagram. At each end hangs the basket, an open-bottomed net, suspended from a ring 3·05 metres (10 feet) above the ground, with a backboard behind it. The basketball is about 760 millimetres (30 inches) around.

The two teams are made up of five players and up to five (in major tournaments up to seven) substitutes each. The players try to gain points by throwing the ball into their opponents' basket. Each goal counts 2 points, unless it is the result of a free throw, when it scores 1 point.

Play begins with a member of each team in the centre circle. The referee throws the ball up, and the two players jump for it, and try to tap it to a team-mate.

Basketball may only be played with the hands – no kicking or hitting the ball with the fist is allowed, unless it is by mistake. You may not run with the ball. You can move with it by dribbling if you want to – you throw it once into the air and then bounce it with the hand. You may take quite a number of steps while doing this and move a long way down the court, but you must not hold the ball with two hands while dribbling. After finishing dribbling you must pass the ball to a team-mate or shoot it at the basket.

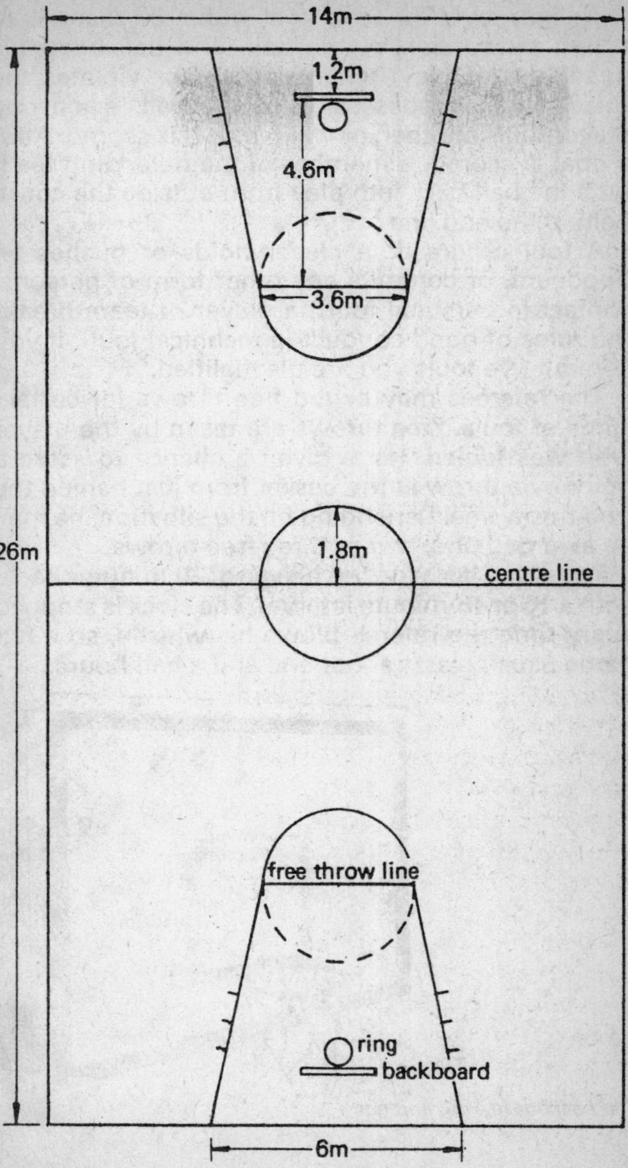
14m
1.2m
4.6m
3.6m
26m
1.8m
centre line
free throw line
ring
backboard
6m

A team must try for a goal within 30 seconds of taking possession of the ball. The ball becomes dead (out of play) when one player violates the rules when in possession of the ball, when one player fouls another, or when a goal is scored. After a goal is scored, a member of the defending team puts the ball back into play from outside the court, behind the end line.

A foul occurs if: a player holds or pushes an opponent, or commits any other form of personal contact (a personal foul); a player or team breaks the rules of good conduct (a technical foul). If you commit five fouls you are disqualified.

The referees may award free throws for certain kinds of fouls. Free throws are taken by the player who was fouled. He is given a chance to score a point by a throw at the basket from just behind the free-throw line. Depending on the situation, he may be awarded one, two or three free throws.

The game lasts for two halves of 20 minutes each, with a 10 or 15 minute interval. The clock is stopped every time the referee blows his whistle, so a full game usually lasts about one and a half hours.

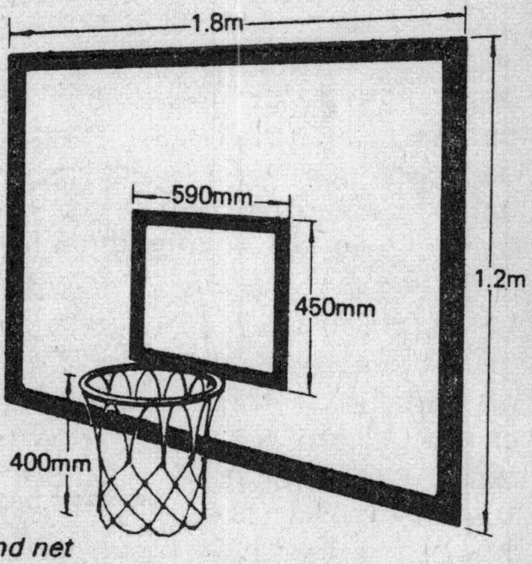

The backboard, ring and net

BILLIARDS

Billiards is the name of two ball games played on a large table covered with green baize. The table has a padded rim called the cushion. The two games are English billiards, played in Britain; and French or Carom billiards, played in France and North and South America. Each game is played by two players. Snooker and Pool are other games played on a billiards table. (See Snooker and Pool).

English Billiards is played on a table with six pockets, one at each corner and one in the middle of each long side. Towards one end is a region called baulk, marked by a line. A D-shaped line marks off part of the baulk. There are four spots down the centre line of the table, one of them on the baulk line. This last spot is flanked by two others. See the diagram.

There are three balls, one red target ball and two white cue balls, one for each player. One white ball is marked with two black spots to identify it. Each player strikes his cue ball with a cue, a long tapered rod with a leather tip.

Game is an agreed number of points. You can score points in three ways. In a winning hazard or pot the cue ball strikes one of the other balls into a pocket. In a losing hazard (also called in-off) the cue ball goes into a pocket after striking one of the other balls. In a cannon the cue ball strikes both the other balls in turn.

To begin the game, you put the red ball on the top spot and the first player's cue ball in the D. You toss a coin to decide who plays first. The second player's ball comes on to the table when his turn arrives. If you pot the red it comes back on to the table, on its spot. If you pot it three times in succession it is placed on the centre spot. If your cue ball goes down it returns to the D; if you put

Standard English billiards table

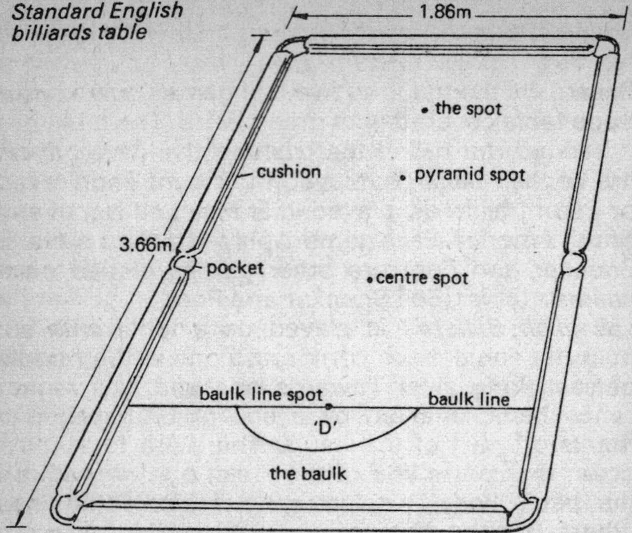

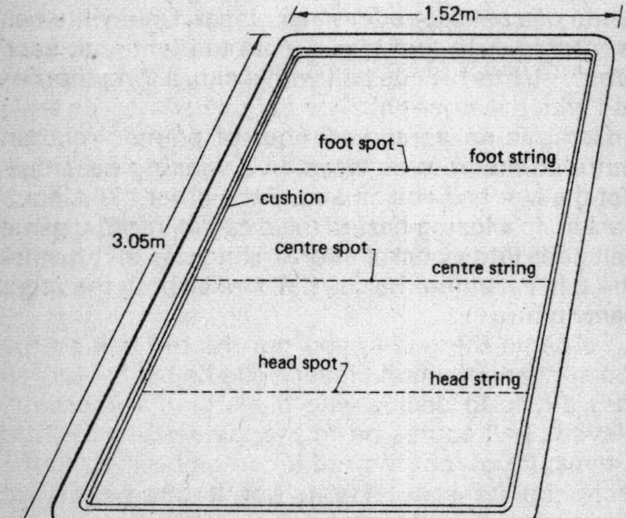

Carom billiards table

your opponent's cue ball down it stays down until his turn comes round again. Your turn, called a break, lasts until you fail to score, when your opponent takes over.

You score 2 points for potting the white, in-off the white, or a cannon; 3 points for potting the red or in-off the red. If you make a combination of any of these you score the combined total of points. If your cue ball fails to hit another ball your opponent scores 1 point; if it goes straight into a pocket he socres 3 points. If the red and opponent's balls are in baulk, you must hit a cushion outside baulk before hitting either of the other balls. The winner is the first player to reach an agreed number of points.

Carom Billiards is played on a table without pockets. The table is marked out with three lines across it, each with a spot in the middle. See the diagram. There is only one scoring stroke, the cannon, called carom (short for the French word for cannon, *carambolage*). The balls and cues used are the same as in English billiards. Play begins with the red ball on the spot at one end of the table and your opponent's ball on the spot at the other. You put your own ball near your opponent's ball. You must begin by striking the red ball first. Each carom counts one point. In a version of the game called three-cushion billiards your cue ball must hit the cushion three times in the course of making a carom.

BOBSLEDDING

Bobsledding or bobsleigh racing is a fast, competitive winter sport for skilled athletes. You are most likely to see it on television. It is a form of tobogganing, only more exciting and dangerous, and is one of the contests in the Winter Olympic Games.

The teams consist of two or four men. They try to cover the course as speedily as possible. Only one bob is allowed on the course at one time.

There are eight bobsleigh tracks in the world. Three – St Moritz (Switzerland), Cortina and Cervinia (Italy) – are made annually from snow, and are 1500 metres (1640 yards) long. The rest are all artificial tracks made of concrete, and they are covered with ice made by refrigeration plants. Four of them – Königsee and Winterberg (West Germany), Igls (Austria) and Sinaia (Rumania) – are

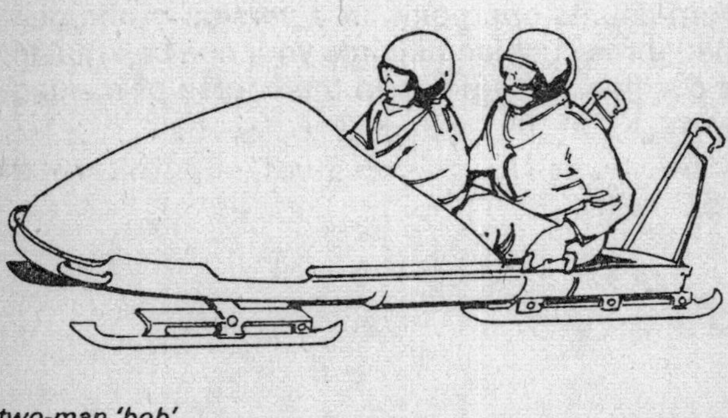

A two-man 'bob'

1200 metres (1300 yards) long; the fifth, Lake Placid (USA), is 1609 metres (1 mile) long. Each track has between 15 and 20 curves in it. The curves are steeply banked with ice-covered walls up to 6 metres (20 feet) high. The course has a slope of between 1 in 12 and 1 in 6.

The captain of the team steers and the rear man controls the brake. The two middle men in a four-man team provide weight and help to control the bob by leaning to one side or the other together. All competitors must wear crash helmets and elbow guards.

The bobs are made of steel, aluminium and glassfibre, and have two pairs of runners. The front runners are mounted on an axle and can be turned for steering. The brake is a toothed bar of steel which can be pressed into the ice to slow down the bob, but as the teeth damage the course, the brakeman only uses it in emergencies.

A two-man bob must not weigh more than 375 kilograms (850 pounds), and a four-man bob must not weigh more than 630 kilograms (1390 pounds) with the men on board, but a team may add ballast to bring it up to the permitted weight level.

At the beginning of a descent a team push their bob off from a point 15 metres (50 feet) behind the starting line, jumping aboard as it gathers speed.

Races consist of four descents of the course by each team. If they crash the run is still valid, so long as they are all on the sled when it reaches the finishing line.

BOWLS

Bowls, called lawn bowling in North America, has been played for at least 700 years in Europe, and a form of it was played in ancient Egypt. The object of the game is to roll a bowl – a large heavy ball – as near as possible to a smaller target ball, the jack. There are two forms of the game, flat green bowls and crown green bowls.

Flat Green Bowls is played in more than twenty countries. The green is a level stretch of lawn 36·5 metres (40 yards) square. It is divided into six rinks or alleys by marks around the edge – the lawn itself is not marked.

The bowls, often called woods, are made of heavy wood or plastic, and are 133 millimetres (5¼ inches) in diameter. They are not completely spherical: one side bulges slightly, giving the bowl a bias – that is, making it roll along the ground in a slightly curving path, instead of straight. They are black or brown in colour. The jack is about half the diameter of the bowls, and is white. It has no bias.

Players use a small black rubber mat, and must keep at least one foot completely on it when bowling. The bowls are delivered underhand, and must be kept close to the ground. Players, umpires and markers must all wear smooth-soled shoes without heels, so that they do not mark the green.

Games are divided into innings called ends, played up and down a rink. In singles two players compete, bowling alternately. Each player has four woods. In doubles, triples and fours there are two, three and four players in each team. In these games the opposing players play in pairs, as in singles. In triples each player has two or three woods; in fours two woods. The first player to play sends down the jack as a target for the game.

In team games fours is the usual number, and the

Flat green bowls

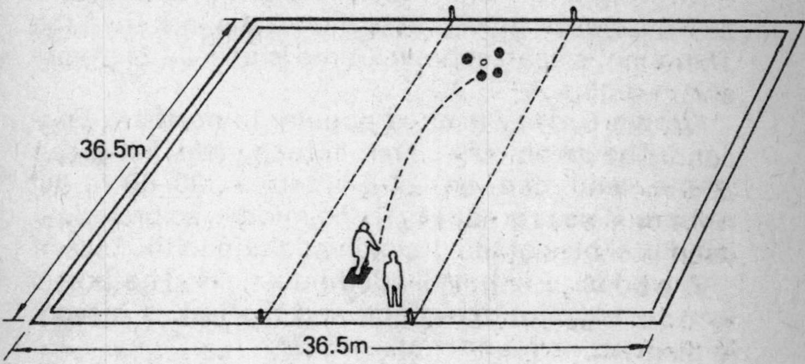

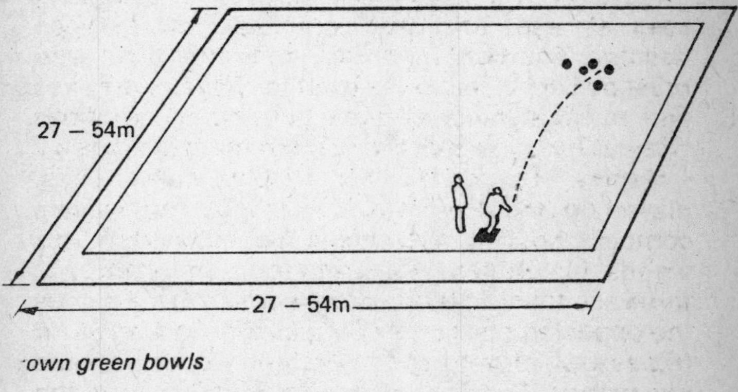

'own green bowls

members of the team are known as lead, second, third and skip (captain). Each has special duties: lead sends down the jack, second keeps the score, third measures any disputed bowls, and skip organises the team effort.

Scoring is simple: the winning player scores 1 point for each bowl that is nearer the jack than the opponent's nearest bowl. Game is usually 21 points (18 in triples).

Crown Green Bowls is popular in northern England. The green may be larger than in the flat-green game, and can be 27–54 metres (30–60 yards) square. It rises gradually to the middle, so providing a natural bias of the green in addition to the bias of the woods. It is not divided into rinks. The bowls can be any size or weight, and the jack is biased. Players use a round mat.

Play is always singles, and each player has two woods. Each end is played across the green in any direction, and a new end is started from a point near where the jack was in the previous end. Scoring is like that of flat-green bowls.

BOXING

Boxing is a contest between two boxers who hit each other with gloved fists. The rules used today are basically those laid down by the 8th Marquess of Queensberry in 1867. They vary slightly from country to country, and between amateur bouts and those boxed by professionals. The rules given here apply to amateurs.

Bouts take place in a roped-off enclosure, the ring, which is between 3·65 and 6 metres (12–20 feet) square. Boxers wear shorts, singlets and boots, and padded leather gloves. Under the gloves their hands are wrapped in soft bandages. Boxers box in classes according to their weights. The classes vary slightly: the weights given in the table opposite are those for international and Olympic amateur contests.

An amateur contest lasts for three 3-minute rounds. There is a one-minute rest between rounds. Inexperienced boxers fight rounds lasting only two minutes each.

Each contest is controlled by a referee, who is in the ring with the boxers. Outside the ring there are three judges. When boxing, you must obey the referee's instructions. You must box cleanly, and not commit fouls, which include hitting your opponent below the belt, on the back of the head, or in the kidneys; hitting your opponent when he is down; hitting your opponent while holding him; butting; and ducking down below waist level.

Victory is won by a knock-out, which occurs when one boxer is knocked down and stays down for at least 10 seconds; by a 'referee stops contest' (R.S.C.) – when the referee decides a boxer is unfit to continue the contest; or on points, which are awarded by the three judges. In some contests the referee is one of the judges. If you are knocked down or fall, but rise again at once, the contest

An amateur boxer

cannot resume until you have taken a compulsory count of eight seconds. If you are knocked down three times in one round, you lose the bout on an R.S.C.

AMATEUR BOXING WEIGHTS

(Olympic and International)

Class	*Kilograms*	*Pounds (lb)*
Heavyweight	Over 81	Over 178
Light heavyweight	Up to 81	Up to 178
Middleweight	Up to 75	Up to 165
Light middleweight	Up to 71	Up to 156
Welterweight	Up to 67	Up to 148
Light welterweight	Up to 63·5	Up to 140
Lightweight	Up to 60	Up to 133
Featherweight	Up to 57	Up to 126
Bantamweight	Up to 54	Up to 119
Flyweight	Up to 51	Up to 112
Light flyweight	Under 49	Under 108

CRICKET

Cricket is a game played between two teams, each of eleven players. The teams take it in turns to bat and field. The batting team tries to make as many runs as possible while the fielding side tries to get the batsmen out. Cricket is England's national summer game, and is equally popular in many Commonwealth and former Commonwealth countries. It was first played at least 680 years ago.

The cricket ground is a large oval, about 150 metres (500 feet) long by 137 metres (450 feet) wide, but the size can vary according to the space available. In the middle is the pitch with the wickets at each end, 20 metres (22 yards) apart. The wickets are made up of three stumps in the ground with two bails resting across them. A white line on the ground level with the stumps is the bowling crease and another line 1·22 metres (4 feet) in front of it is the popping crease.

Cricket bats are made of wood from the willow tree, and must not be longer than 965 millimetres (38 inches) and 108 millimetres (4¼ inches) wide. The ball is covered with leather and has a raised stitched seam which can be used to make the ball spin.

Each team has two innings, taken alternately. (One innings each may be played by agreement). Two batsmen play at a time, each guarding a wicket. The fielding side bowls from each end in turn in overs of 6 or 8 balls, as agreed before the match. Members of the bowling side stand around the pitch to field the ball. The positions of the fieldsmen and umpires are not laid down in the laws of cricket, but the diagram shows the possible placings of fieldsmen opposing a right-handed batsman. Positions are reversed for a left-handed batsman.

A run is scored when the batsmen run between the wickets after the ball is bowled, whether a

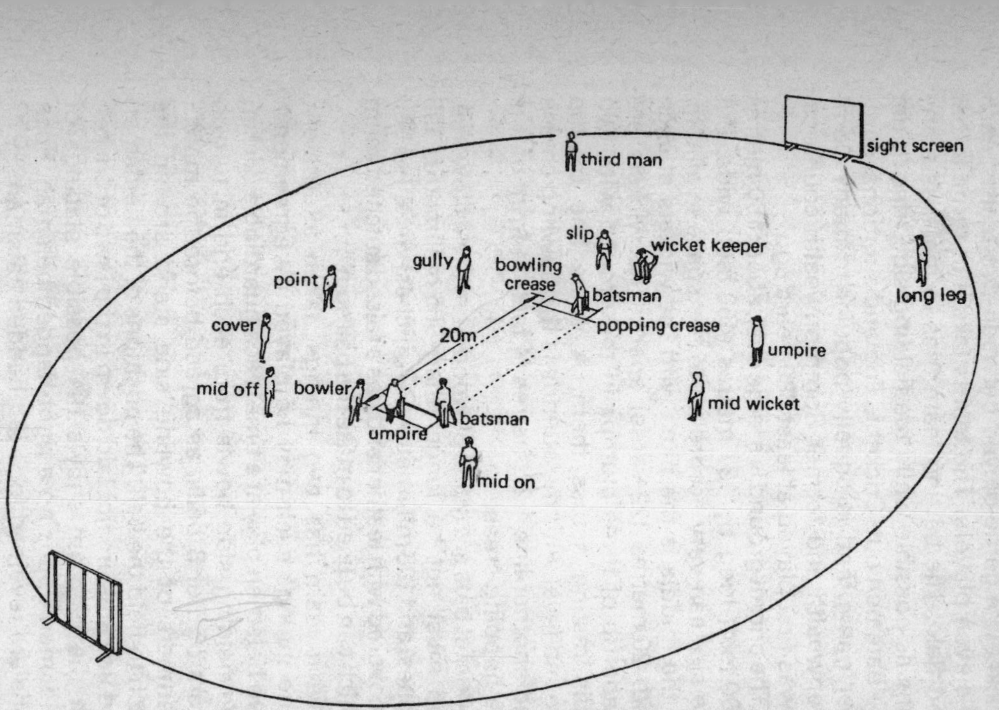

Possible fielding positions for a right-handed batsman

batsman hits it or not. A bye is scored if the batsmen run without having hit the ball. The batsmen may run as many times as they can. If the ball is hit and rolls or bounces across the boundary 4 runs are scored; if it flies across the boundary without touching the ground it scores 6 runs. A lost ball also scores 6 runs.

The ball must be bowled, not thrown. This means that the ball must be delivered overarm with all the movement coming from the shoulder, not from the elbow. A skilful bowler uses his wrist and fingers to make the ball turn in the air. The bowler must have his front foot behind the popping crease as he lets go of the ball, otherwise the umpire calls 'no-ball'. If the ball is out of reach of the batsman it is declared a wide and one run is scored even if the batsmen do not actually run.

A batsman is out if the ball, or his bat or body, knocks either bail off the stumps. If he is out of his ground – that is, having no part of his bat or body touching the ground behind the popping crease, any player may knock off the bails and the batsman is out. He is also out if he hits the ball with his bat or hand and a fieldsman then catches it before it touches the ground. He is out 'Leg before wicket', (usually shortened to 'LBW') if he blocks the ball with his body before he hits it with his bat, and the umpire decides that the ball would have struck the wicket if the batsman had not got in the way.

An innings ends when 10 of the 11 batsmen are out. The side which scores the most runs in the match wins. The winning side may not need to finish its second innings. If the side which bats first leads by 75 runs in a one-day match (more in longer matches) after the second team has completed its first innings, the first team may require the second team to 'follow on' – that is, to take its second innings right away.

CROQUET

Association croquet is a game for two or four people. The players try to hit composition balls with a mallet through a series of hoops, which are spaced out on a smooth, level lawn.

The lawn should be 32 metres long by 25·6 metres wide (35×28 yards). An inner rectangle is shown by corner pegs; its unmarked lines are called yard-lines because they are 910 millimetres (1 yard) inside the boundary. An 11·9-metre (13-yard) section to the left of each of the shorter yard-lines is called a baulk-line.

The hoops are made of iron and are placed as shown on the diagram. There is also a wooden peg 460 millimetres (18 inches) high. The mallets are made of wood, sometimes strengthened with metal, and have long handles. There are four different coloured balls 92 millimetres (3⅝ inches) across: blue, red, black and yellow. (Brown, green, pink and white are also allowed.)

When four people play, each player takes one ball. When there are only two players they take two balls each. Blue and black are partners against red and yellow. The players toss a coin to decide who shall play first, then play alternately.

Play begins with each ball on a baulk-line. Each player sends his ball through the hoops in the order shown on the diagram, ending by striking the peg in the middle. Each hoop and the peg counts one point. Each player's turn lasts one stroke, unless he manages to send his ball through a hoop, when he is allowed to play a second stroke, called a continuation shot.

A player can also earn another stroke by making a roquet – that is, by hitting one of the other three balls with his own ball. Following a roquet he places his ball so that it touches the roqueted ball, and hits it so that his own ball rolls towards the next hoop or another ball. This is the croquet shot, and it is followed by a continuation shot. A player is entitled to roquet only once after going through a hoop.

A ball that goes over the yard-line is out of play and must be placed back on the yard-line opposite where it went off.

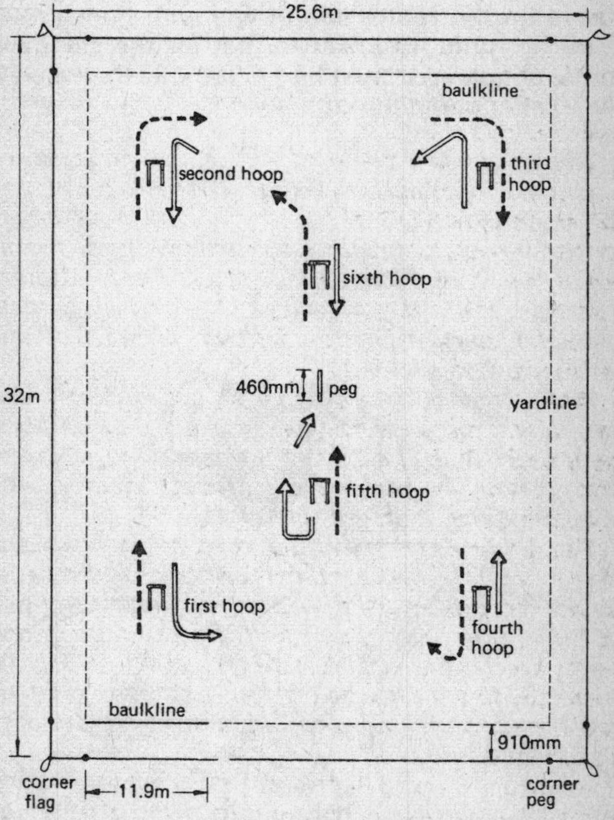

A croquet lawn: the dotted arrows show the direction of play at the start of the game; the solid arrows show the return journey – through twelve hoops altogether.

Golf Croquet is played round the same course, but the peg is not used. Players decide between a 13 or a 19 point game, and the first one to score most of the points wins. Each turn consists of only one stroke, without roquet, croquet or continuation shots, and the point is secured by the player whose ball first goes through the hoop.

Older versions of croquet include two pegs, placed on the centre line in line with hoops 1–4, 2–3. The route is similar to that for the standard game, but players must hit the top peg (between 2 and 3) after going through hoop 6.

A track cyclist

CYCLE RACING

Cycle racing is a sport almost as old as the bicycle itself, and forms part of the Olympic Games. There are two main kinds of races: track races and road races, with several varieties of both.

Track cycles have no brakes, gears or freewheel, so they have to be pedalled all the time. Cycles used for road events are more like ordinary bicycles – they have gears and must have brakes. Competitors must wear crash helmets for both road and track races.

Tracks are of a banked oval shape, and surfaced in timber, concrete or asphalt. Track races may be over a distance, or against the clock, such as in the kilometre time trial, when competitors set off at one minute intervals to cover a set distance in the shortest possible time. Pacing of competitors is allowed in track races. The pacer is a non-competitor who rides just in front of a competitor to give him shelter. The pacer is either a tandem bicycle team or a solo motorcyclist. Motorcycles have to be fitted with a roller 600 millimetres (24 inches) wide behind them to prevent the following cycle from getting too close. This prevents the cyclist from receiving too much shelter or reaching a dangerously fast speed.

Road races take place on closed circuits or public roads. When the races are on public roads the riders must obey the traffic laws of the country where the race is held.

Competitors have to be members of recognised cycle clubs. Riders must not help one another (except by pacing) or deliberately hamper each other. They are not allowed to take special drugs to help them ride faster and carry on longer, but they are permitted to take food and drink handed to them while they race.

DARTS

Darts is a target game at least 400 years old. It is particularly popular in the British Isles, though it is also played in other parts of the world – the Pilgrim Fathers took it to America in 1620.

Each player has three darts to throw at a dartboard which is hung with its centre 1·73 metres (5 feet 8 inches) from the floor. The standard dartboard is shown in the picture. Darts which land in each segment score its value, but if they land in the narrow outer ring they score double; if in the narrow ring nearer the middle, treble. The bullseye in the centre scores 50, and the small ring around it, called the inner, 25.

Players throw their darts from behind a world-recognised throwing line 2·37 metres (7 feet 9¼ inches) from the board.

The standard darts game is played between individual players or by teams. The target score is usually 301 or 501, and the chosen score number is chalked up on the scoreboard before play begins. The players' individual totals are deducted from this number until zero is reached.

Players throw their darts in turn, and players must end on a double. The highest possible score during one turn is 180 (three darts in the treble 20). If a player aiming for a finishing double scores more than he needs to reach zero, his turn ends and his target score stays the same. The lowest possible finishing score is 2 (double 1); the highest is bullseye (double 25). Darts that miss the board, bounce out or lodge in other darts do not count.

Other games include Round the Clock, Cricket and Killer. In Round the Clock players must throw one dart into each sector in turn, starting with 1 (it does not matter if the darts land in the double or treble rings). In Cricket players form two teams. The

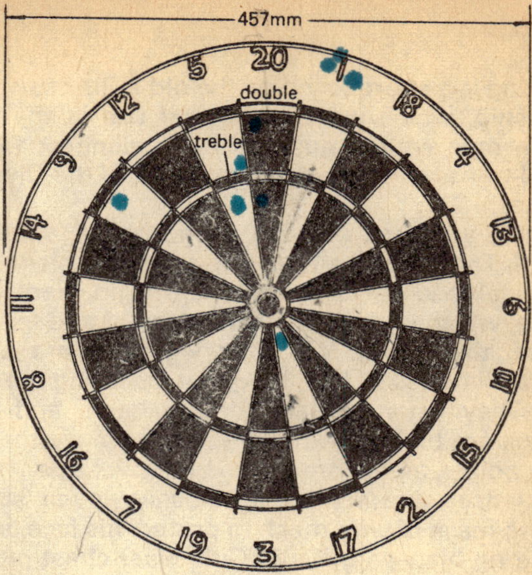

The standard dart board

'bowlers' take 'wickets' by hitting the bullseye. 'Batsmen' score what they make as 'runs'; in some versions of this game the 'batsmen' can count only the amount they score over 41 with any three darts. In Killer each player throws a dart left-handed (or right-handed if he is naturally left-handed) to decide which sector is his. He then has three 'lives'. He must start by throwing a double of his own number, and is then 'licensed to kill'. He takes his opponents' lives by throwing darts into their sectors. A double takes two lives, and a treble takes three lives. The last player with a 'life' left wins.

FENCING

Fencing is a sport based on the old skills of swordsmanship, which were in general use in the days when men settled quarrels by duelling or fought hand-to-hand in battle. It forms part of the Olympic Games.

There are three kinds of weapons: foil, epée and sabre. The foil has a four-sided, flexible blade. The heavier epée has a three-sided, rigid blade. The sabre, which is about the same weight as a foil, has a flat, thin blade. All three weapons are about 900 millimetres (3 feet) long, not including the handle. They have a guard for the hand, and their blades are blunt. Foils and epées have buttons on their points, and sabres have bent-over tips.

A fencer wears a white, closely-woven suit, a strong mask of wire mesh to protect his face, and a glove on his sword hand. Girls wear chest protectors as well.

A bout lasts until one fencer has scored five hits. The time limit is 6 minutes. Hits must be scored on the target area, which varies according to whether you are using foil, epée or sabre. The picture shows you the target areas.

There are three basic moves in fencing: attack, parry (warding off the attack) and riposte (an offensive movement following the parry). In foil and sabre fencing the defender must parry before he may make a riposte.

Fencing takes place on an area called a piste, a long, narrow strip of floor, and you must not step off it. You must also avoid body-to-body contact.

In competition fencing a president and four judges control the bouts, or, if electronic scoring apparatus is used, just a president.

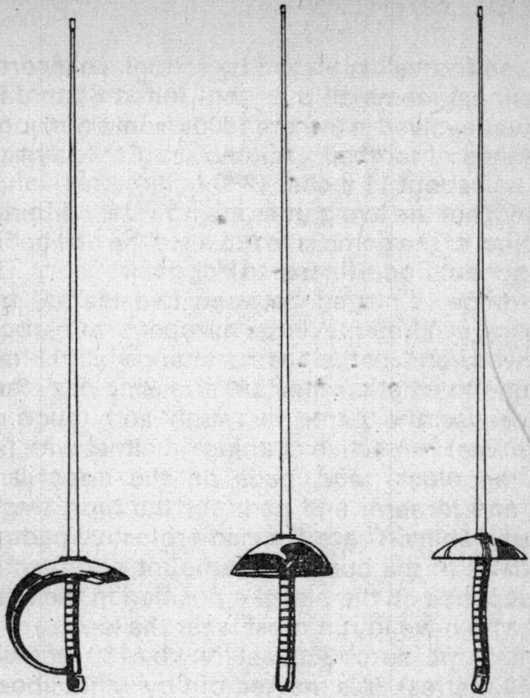

sabre epée foil

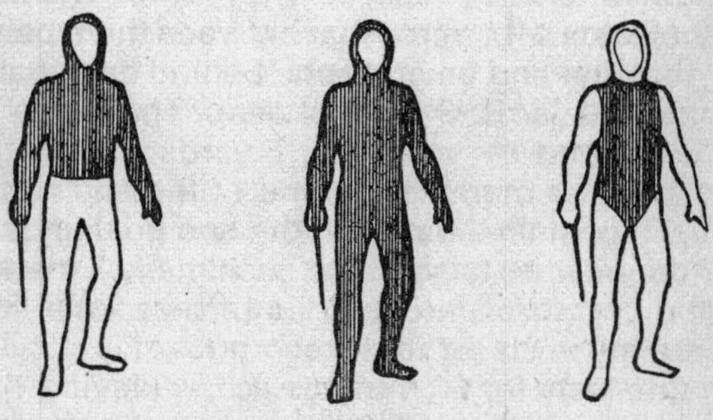

target areas

FOOTBALL: AMERICAN

American football is played by school, college and professional teams all over the United States. The game was evolved in the late 1800s from a number of other kinds of football, including rugby football. A rugby ball about 11 inches (280 millimetres) long is still used, but the two games are now very different. The object of the game is to advance the ball behind the opponents' goal line, or to kick goals.

The game is played between two teams, each consisting of 11 men. A large number of substitutes is allowed, and some teams change all 11 men according to whether they are attacking or defending. Because the game is rough and tough, all players wear protective clothing – helmet with face guard, shoulder pads, pads on the upper arm, elbow and forearm and pads for the hips, thighs, knees and shins. There are also protective pads for other parts of the body. The amount of protection worn depends on the player's position in the team. Those who have to run most wear the least.

The field measures 360 feet long by 160 feet wide (110×49 metres). It is marked out by white lines in a gridiron pattern, from which comes the popular name for a football field, 'the gridiron'. There are two goalposts with a crossbar between them behind each goal line and an end zone behind each pair of goalposts 10 yards (9 metres) deep. The rest of the field is divided by yardlines, 5 yards (4·6 metres) apart. The line marking the end of the end zone is called the goal line. Between the two goal lines are two inbound lines (also called hash marks), marking the field into three equal strips (professional hash lines are much closer to the centre).

A game lasts for 60 minutes actual playing time, but with time allowed for stoppages and other interruptions the total time is nearer two hours. It is

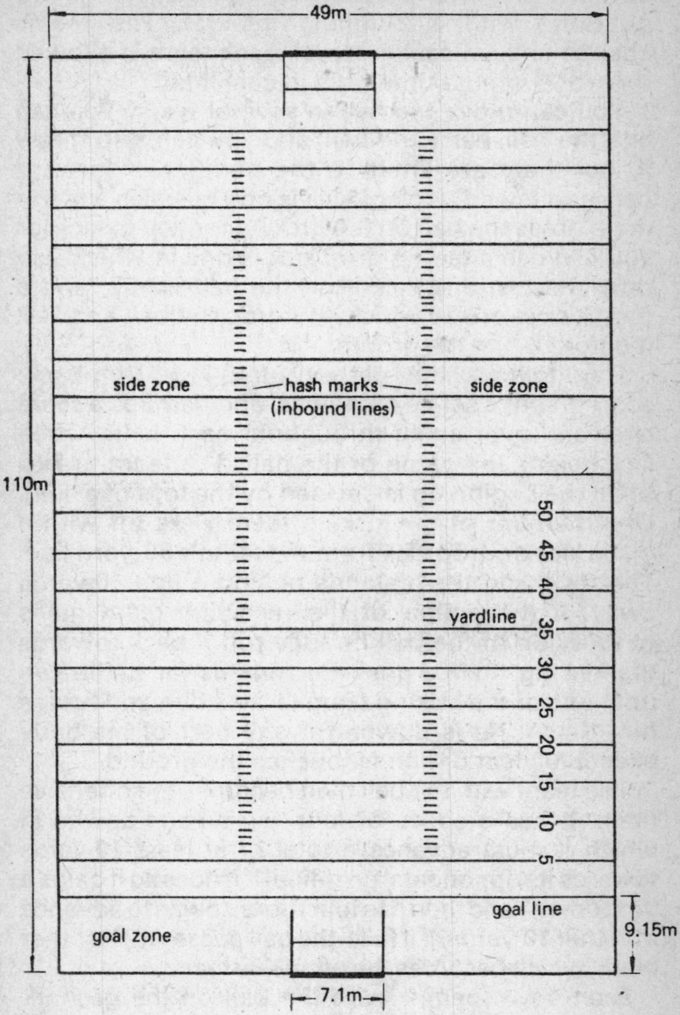
49m
side zone
hash marks
(inbound lines)
side zone
110m
50
45
40
yardline
35
30
25
20
15
10
5
goal line
9.15m
goal zone
7.1m

divided into two halves, with a 15-minute interval between them, and each half is divided into two quarters, with a 2-minute interval. The teams change ends at each interval. Each team is allowed three 1½-minute time-outs in each half.

You can move the ball in several ways. You can kick the ball, carry the ball, and you can also throw it, but there are limits to the number of forward passes allowed. A place kick is one in which a team-mate holds the ball on the ground for you to kick (or you can use a tee); a drop kick is one in which you drop the ball and kick it on the half-volley; and a punt kick is one in which you drop the ball and kick it before it hits the ground.

Play follows the pattern: free-kick; run-back; scrimmage; a series of 'downs' and perhaps a score over and over again throughout each half. A free kick begins the game or the half. The team to kick off at the beginning is decided by the toss of a coin. One member of the kicking team kicks off with a place kick or drop kick from the team's 35-yard line. The receiving team stands behind a line 10 yards away. If a member of the receiving team gains possession of the ball he may run it back towards the kicking team's goal. He runs as far as he can until one of the kicking team tackles him and brings him down. He is downed if any part of his body except his feet or hands touches the ground.

The team with the ball then becomes the offensive team. It has a series of four scrimmage-downs in which it must advance a total of at least 10 yards towards its opponents' goal-line. If it does so it gains a 'first down', and then has four more downs to advance a further 10 yards. If it fails, the ball passes to the other team, which becomes the offensive team.

Each down begins with the ball on the ground. The two teams line up facing each other along the scrimmage lines. These imaginary lines run parallel

Protective clothing worn for American football

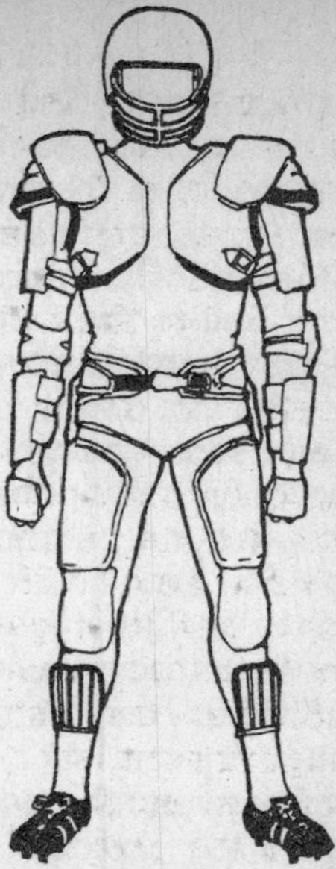

to the yardlines, and through the two tips of the ball. The offensive team must have at least seven men along the scrimmage line, known as linemen. The usual arrangement is a centre, with two linemen either side of him, called guards. The two linemen beyond the guards are called tackles, and the men at the ends of the line are called ends. Behind the linemen are the backfield men – a quarterback, two halfbacks and a fullback. The defensive line-up varies, but usually has at least four linemen, several linebackers standing just behind them, and four backs. The centre begins play with a snap – passing the ball back between his legs to the quarterback. The quarterback or one of the other backs then runs forward as far as he can before he is downed by a tackle. Any player can make a lateral pass – that is, one in which the ball moves sideways or back – but only the four backs can make a forward pass, and only the two ends, or a player who was standing at least 3 yards (2·7 metres) behind the scrimmage line, can catch it. The other linemen must stay behind the scrimmage line until the pass is made. If the ball touches the ground before being caught, it is dead. Instead of carrying the ball forward on a down, the offensive team may punt it forward. This gives the ball to their opponents, but with a territorial advantage to the punting team, and is usually done on the last down.

You can score points in four ways. You score a touchdown (worth 6 points) when the ball is touched on to the ground behind the opponents' goal-line. A defensive player can score a touchdown if he catches the ball in play and runs with it. When you have made a touchdown, your team can try for an extra point, or conversion. You convert by kicking the ball from at least the 3-yard line over the crossbar between the goalposts, and score 1 point. You can also score the extra point from another touchdown or a safety. You can score a field goal by place-kicking the ball over the crossbar from anywhere on the field. This is worth 3 points. The defensive team can score a safety, worth 2 points, if the offensive player carrying the ball is downed in his own end zone. The team with most points wins the game.

If the ball goes out of play it is put back again by a scrimmage from the nearest point on the hash marks. In some circumstances play restarts with a kick-off.

If a team breaks the rules penalties are awarded against it. Sometimes they are the loss of yardage – 5, 10 or 15 yards; sometimes the loss of a down. Play is controlled by a referee, assisted by an umpire who stands behind the defensive line; a head linesman who stands at one end of the scrimmage line; and a field judge who stands at the other end of the line, and also times the game. There may also be a back judge and a line judge.

FOOTBALL: ASSOCIATION

Association football, or 'soccer' as it is often called, is the most popular game in the world. It is the national game of many European and South American countries, and is widely played in Asia, Africa and Australasia. It is rapidly gaining ground in North America, too. It is the oldest of the football games. A form of football was played in England in the Middle Ages, and the rules of Association football as we know it today were finally drawn up in the 1800s.

The game is normally played between two teams of 11 players. The object of the game is to send the ball into your opponents' goal. The winning team is the one which scores more goals. Only the goalkeepers can handle the ball: the other players can move the ball with any parts of their bodies except the hands or arms.

Association football is played on a rectangular field. The long side of the field must be not less than 90 metres (100 yards) and not more than 120 metres (130 yards), and the short side should be between 45 and 90 metres (50–100 yards). It is marked out as shown on the diagram. The goals consist of two upright posts 7·3 metres (8 yards) apart connected by a crossbar 2·4 metres (8 feet) from the ground. The ball is round. Players of each team wear uniform clothing (shorts, shirt and boots or shoes), but the goalkeepers must wear colours which distinguish them from the other players. The game is controlled by a referee, assisted by two linesmen who patrol the sidelines of the pitch, out of the field of play.

A game normally lasts for two halves of 45 minutes, with an interval of five minutes during which the teams change ends. The referee can add on time for injury or other interruptions of play at the end of

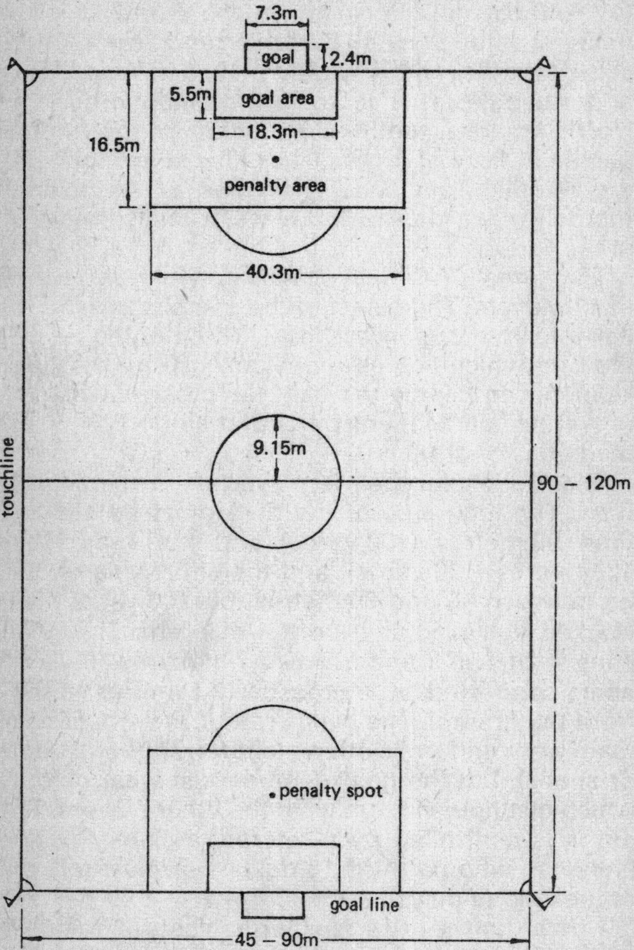
7.3m
goal
2.4m
5.5m
goal area
18.3m
16.5m
penalty area
40.3m
9.15m
touchline
90 – 120m
penalty spot
goal line
45 – 90m

each half. Substitutes are allowed, the number depending on the type of match.

Before the game the teams toss a coin to decide which shall have choice of ends or kick-off. The winning team can choose either which end it wants, or to kick off. Play begins with the ball on the centre spot. When the referee gives the signal to start one of the players kicks the ball forward. Play starts in the same way after half-time, and after a goal has been scored. At half-time the kick-off is taken by the team which did not begin the game; after a goal the team which lost the goal kicks off. You score goals by sending the ball between the goal posts and under the crossbar.

When the ball goes out of play over one of the touch lines (sidelines), it is thrown in by a player of the team opposite to that of the player who last touched the ball. When throwing-in, you hold the ball with both hands and throw it from behind and over your head. When the ball goes out of play over one of the goal lines, it can be put back into play in two ways. If the last person to touch the ball was a member of the team attacking the goal, a goal kick is taken. A player of the defending side (usually the goalkeeper) kicks it into play from within the goal area (see diagram). If the last person to touch the ball was a member of the defending team, a corner-kick is taken. The ball is placed in the quarter-circle by the nearest corner-post, and is kicked into play by a member of the attacking team.

The off-side rule is designed to prevent players from taking up an unfairly advantageous position. Basically, a player is off-side if, at the moment the ball is played by a team-mate, he is nearer his opponents' goal line than two members of the opposing team. There are some exceptions: the rule does not apply if you are in your own half of the field; you receive the ball direct from a

goal-kick, a corner-kick, or a throw-in; or the ball is dropped by the referee. The penalty is an indirect free-kick awarded to the opposing side.

There are a number of things you must not do, which are regarded as fouls or misconduct. You must not kick, trip, strike, or jump at an opponent; charge him violently or from behind; hold him; or handle the ball (unless you are a goalkeeper within your own penalty area). The punishment for doing any of these things is a direct free-kick awarded to the other side. Obstruction and dangerous play are penalised by the award of an indirect free-kick. Goalkeepers must not take more than four steps while holding, bouncing or throwing the ball in the air, or waste time. Such conduct also draws an indirect free-kick.

The various penalties are taken as follows: A direct free-kick is taken from the spot where the foul or other misconduct occurred. You may score a goal from it if you can. An indirect free-kick is taken in the same way, but you cannot score a goal directly from it – the ball must touch another person first. When you take a free-kick all opposing players must be at least 9 metres (10 yards) from the ball, unless they are standing on their own goal-line between the goal-posts.

A penalty kick is awarded for a foul by a defender inside the penalty area (see diagram). It is taken from the penalty spot opposite the goal mouth, and only the goalkeeper is allowed to defend it. All other players must be outside the penalty area and at least 9 metres (10 yards) from the penalty spot. The goalkeeper must stand on his own goal line and must not move his feet until the ball is kicked.

In addition to these penalties, the referee may caution a player for bad behaviour, and in serious cases may send him off the field. He takes no further part in the game, and his team cannot send on a substitute for him.

Several small variations of the rules are allowed by agreement between the teams and the referee, except in certain competitions. If the game is drawn when time is up, extra time may be played, usually in two 15-minute halves, with the players changing ends at half-time.

FOOTBALL: AUSTRALIAN RULES

Australian Rules football is a fast game played only in Australia and Papua-New Guinea. It was developed in the 1840s, and the first code of rules was drawn up in 1860. It is played on an oval pitch. Each team has 18 players in it, plus two substitutes. The ball is long and oval.

The pitch is between 135 and 185 metres long, and 110 and 155 metres wide. It is marked out as shown in the diagram, which also shows the positions of the players when play begins. The game lasts for 100 minutes, divided into four quarters. The interval between the first and second quarters is 3 minutes; that between second and third is 20 minutes; and that between third and fourth is 5 minutes. The teams change ends at each interval. Time when the ball is out of play or after a goal has been scored is waste time, and does not count towards the 100 minutes.

In play, you can kick the ball, and you can carry it and run with it. When running with the ball you must bounce it or touch it on the ground at least every 10 metres. You cannot throw it to another player, but you can pass it by hitting it with your clenched fist. You can tackle, between shoulders and knees, an opponent who has the ball. If a team-mate has the ball you can block or 'shepherd' an opponent within 4·5 metres of him.

Scoring is by points, and the team with the most points wins. There is a goal at each end of the oval, marked by tall posts. Shorter posts, called behind posts, stand on each side of the goal posts (see diagram). You score 6 points for a goal – that is, if you kick the ball between the goal posts without its touching either of them or another player. If the ball hits a goal post or goes between a goal post and a behind post it counts as a behind, and you score 1

The Australian Rules football pitch with one team in position

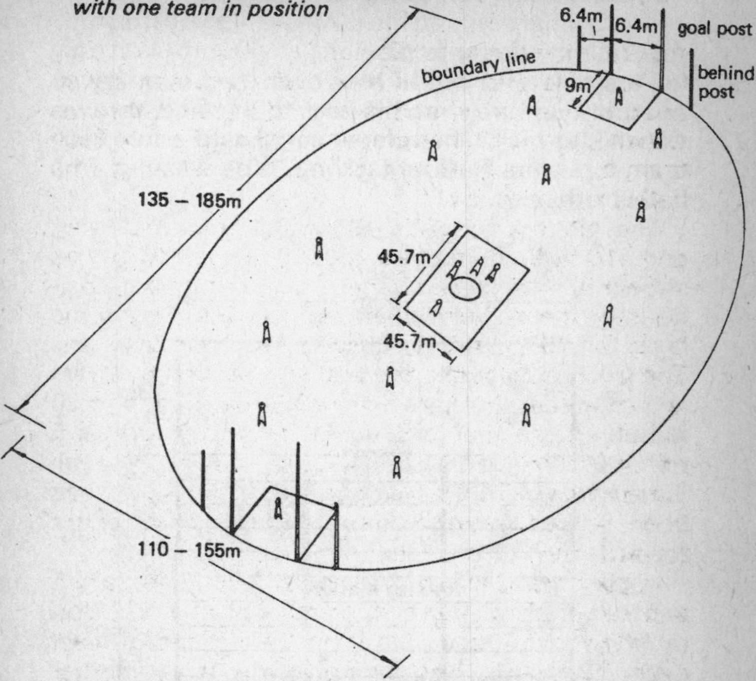

point. If the ball passes directly over a goal post or touches another player before passing between the goal posts, it is also counted as a behind.

The game is controlled by two field umpires. They are assisted by four other umpires, one behind each goal and one behind each side boundary line. There are also two timekeepers. One of the field umpires starts the game by bouncing the ball in the centre of the field. They restart the game in the same way after each interval and each goal. After a behind, a member of the defending team kicks the ball back into play from the box in front of his goal.

You 'mark' a ball by catching it from the kick of another player, who must be at least 10 metres off.

If you mark the ball you are entitled to a free kick from anywhere behind the place where you marked. But you may prefer to play on.

If the ball goes out of play over the boundary, a boundary umpire, with his back to the field, throws it back into play. The referee can award a free kick against players for foul tackling, time wasting and similar offences.

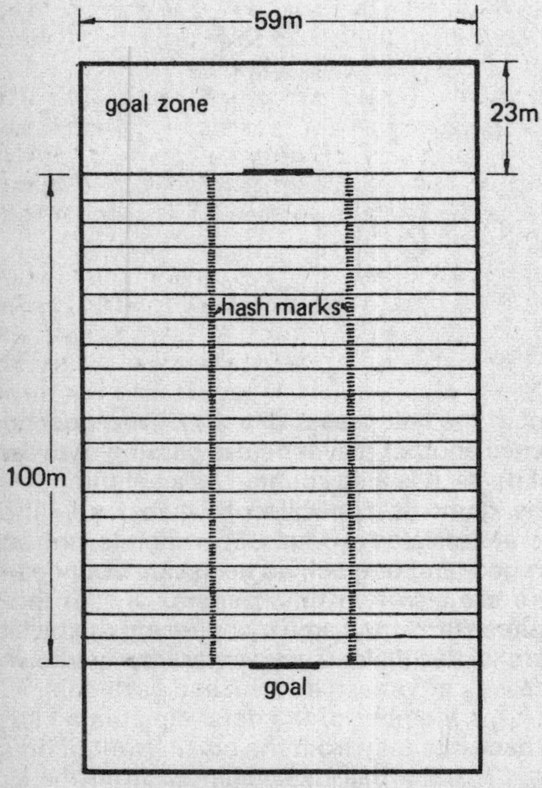

The Canadian football pitch

FOOTBALL: CANADIAN

Canadian football, like American football, is derived from rugby football. It is now very similar indeed to American football, and there are only a few – though important – differences between the two games.

The first difference is that the pitch is bigger: it is longer – 100 metres (330 feet) – and wider – 59 metres (195 feet) – than the American pitch. The goal posts are on the goal line, and there is a very deep dead-ball or goal zone extending 23 metres (25 yards) behind the goal line.

The second major difference between the two games is that each team consists of 12 men instead of 11. The extra man plays in the backfield, either as a flying wing or a flanker. The offensive team is allowed only 3 downs, instead of 4, to advance the ball 10 yards.

Scoring is the same in both games, except that there is an extra way of scoring in Canadian football, called a rouge or single point. If the offensive team plays the ball over the defensive team's deadline, or if they tackle the receiver of a kick in his own end zone, they score a rouge (1 point). The conversion attempt after a touchdown is made from the 5-yard line.

The scrimmage line is slightly different, too. The offensive team's scrimmage line is in line with the nearest point of the ball, as in the American game, but the defensive team's scrimmage line is 900 millimetres (1 yard) away from it, instead of just the length of the ball. Team time-outs are not allowed.

FOOTBALL: RUGBY

Rugby football is a tough, fast game which takes its name from Rugby School in England. In the early days of football there were no standard rules, and each school adopted its own. In a match at Rugby in 1823 a boy named William Webb Ellis picked up the ball and ran with it, thus beginning the distinctive feature of rugby and the games derived from it. Today rugby is played with an oval ball, which is easier to handle than a round one. Scoring is by points, and the team which has the most points wins. There are two basic kinds of rugby football; Rugby Union, which is the amateur game, and Rugby League, which is a professional game you may be able to watch.

Rugby Union is played between two teams of 15 players, on a field not more than 100 metres (110 yards) long by 68 metres (75 yards) wide. It is marked out as shown in the diagram. The goals consist of two very tall posts 5·6 metres (18 feet 6 inches) apart, connected by a crossbar 3 metres (10 feet) from the ground. In international matches two substitutes are allowed, but only for players who are injured.

Play begins with a kick-off from the centre spot. There are three ways of kicking the ball. In a drop kick you let the ball drop from your hands, and kick it as it bounces; in a punt you let the ball drop and kick it before it reaches the ground; in a place kick you put the ball on the ground and then kick it. You may tackle a player who is holding the ball, by holding him so that he cannot play the ball or pass it to another player. You may pass the ball by throwing it to another player, but you must not throw it forwards towards your opponents' goal. For this reason all passes are made to a player slightly behind you.

The game is controlled by a referee, and two touch judges who decide whether a ball has gone out of touch (out of play).

There are four ways of scoring. A try, worth 4 points, is scored if you touch the ball on to the ground in your opponents' goal area, the ground immediately behind the line of the goal posts. (You can also score on the line.) This is called grounding the ball. When you have scored a try you can attempt a conversion – that is, a place kick or drop kick at goal. This is worth 2 points. A dropped goal, worth 3 points, is scored during play by a drop kick. To make a goal, the ball must go over the crossbar between the posts. If you are awarded a free kick as a penalty against your opponents, you can make a penalty goal from it (3 points). The referee may also award a penalty try if a try was foiled by foul play on the part of the defenders.

The referee may order a scrummage (or scrum) when there has been an infringement of the rules. In a scrummage, the forwards from each side close around the ball, or form a tunnel so that the ball can be put in between them. There must be three players in the front row. A player from the non-offending side puts the ball into the scrummage. The players then try to hook the ball out with their feet. Players in a scrummage must hold together by putting an arm or arms around their team-mates. A ruck is formed when players from both teams who are on their feet close around the ball when it is on the ground and in play; a maul is formed when players close around another player who is carrying the ball.

If the ball goes out of play over the touch lines (see diagram), a line-out is formed. Players from the two teams form a pair of parallel lines at right angles to the touch line. Only players within 15 metres of the touch line can take part. The

Rugby Union pitch

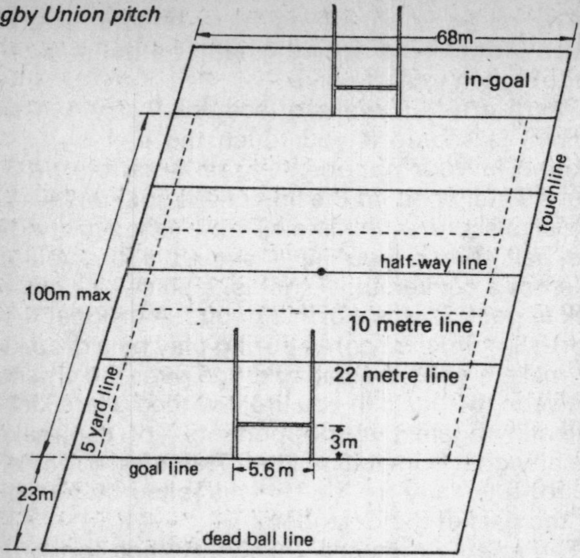

Rugby League pitch

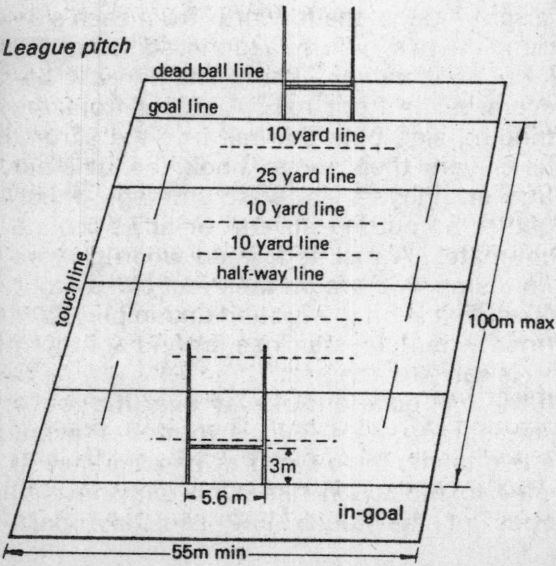

line-out begins 5 metres from the touch line. The ball is thrown between the two lines of players, who attempt to catch it. You can also make a quick throw-in without waiting for the line-out to be formed.

You are deemed to be off-side if you are in front of a team-mate who is playing or carrying the ball, but there is no penalty unless you play the ball or obstruct an opponent. You can also be off-side during a scrummage if you join it from the wrong side, or fail to keep clear if you are not in it. There are similar rules for mauls and rucks, and for line-outs.

You can tackle a player who is carrying the ball by charging him with the shoulder or throwing your arms around him, but you must not strike, kick or trip him – and you must not tackle a player who does not have the ball. You must not knock-on – that is, knock the ball towards your opponents' goal-line with your hand or arm. After a tackle, the ball is put back into play by a scrummage.

Rugby League, the professional game, was started in the 1890s. The basic rules of play are similar to those of Rugby Union, with a few important differences. There are only 13 players, a League team having six forwards instead of eight. The field is the same size, but is marked out slightly differently (see diagram). The ball is slightly smaller. Substitutes are allowed for reasons other than injury.

Scoring is slightly different: 3 points for a try; 2 points for a conversion (which must be a place kick); 1 point for a drop goal; 2 points for a penalty goal. After a tackle, the ball may be put back into play by a play-the-ball – the tackled player stands up, faces his opponents' goal and drops the ball on the ground in front of him. There is no line-out, but if the ball goes out of play over the touch lines it is put back into play with a scrummage. A scrummage is also called after three successive play-the-balls.

Rugby League Team		Rugby Union Team	
Players sometimes wear their respective numbers on the backs of their jerseys			
1	Full-back	1	Prop forward
2	Right wing three-quarter	2	Hooker
3	Right centre three-quarter	3	Prop forward
4	Left centre three-quarter	4	Lock forward
5	Left wing three-quarter	5	Lock forward
6	Stand-off half	6	Flank forward
7	Scrum-half	7	Flank forward
8	Front row prop forward	8	No. 8 forward
9	Hooker	9	Scrum-half back
10	Front row forward	10	Stand-off half-back
11	Second row forward	11	Left wing three-quarter back
12	Second row forward	12	Left centre three-quarter back
		13	Right centre three-quarter back
13	Loose forward		
14	Reserve back (substitute)	14	Right wing three-quarter back
15	Reserve forward (substitute)	15	Full back

GOLF

Golf is one of the most popular games and also one of the oldest. The Romans played a similar game, and it was revived in Scotland in the twelfth century.

The object of the game is to hit a ball around a course into a series of holes – 18 for a full round, 9 for a half round. The player who does this in the fewest strokes wins. In match play the strokes for each hole are counted separately, and the player who wins the most holes is the victor. In stroke or medal play the total number of strokes taken for all the holes is added up, and the player with the lowest total wins.

The basic rules are very simple. You must use standard golf balls and clubs, and you must not take more than 14 clubs round the course with you. You choose which club to use at each stroke, depending on what sort of ground the ball has

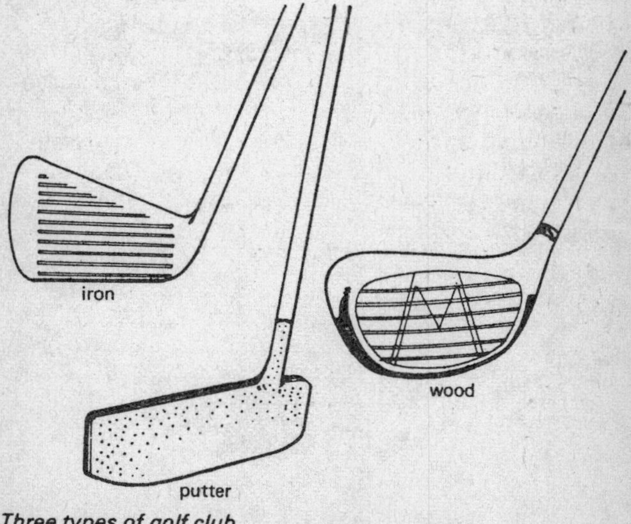

Three types of golf club

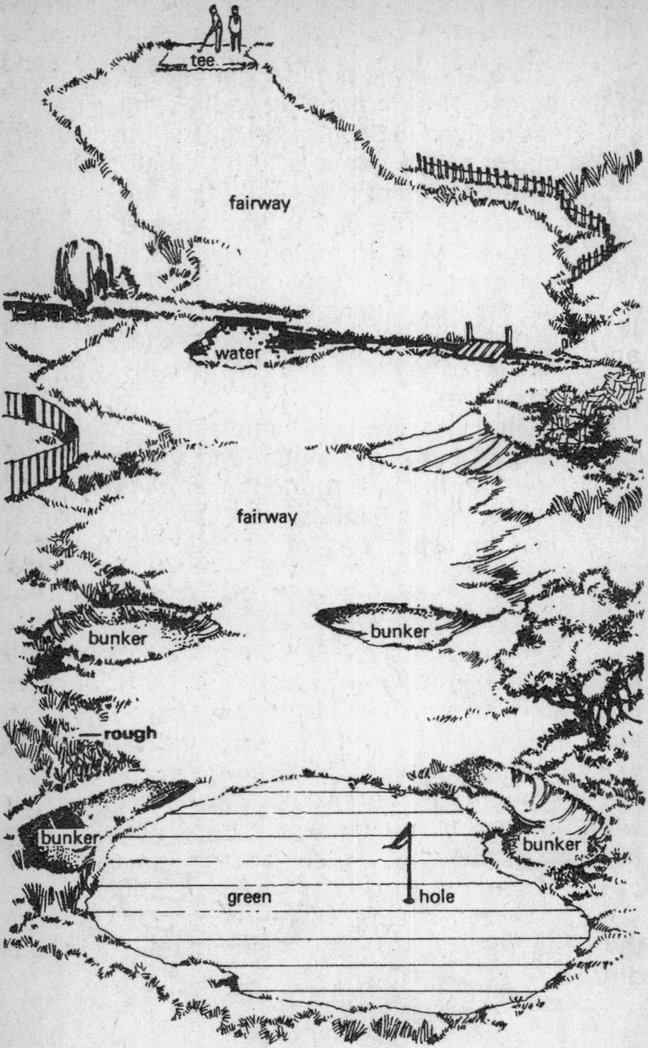

A typical golf hole, with a variety of hazards

landed on. Golfers use a wood to drive off from the tee at the start of each hole to send the ball as far as possible down the fairway, and an iron to send the ball high out of the rough or a bunker. When the ball reaches the green, the putter is the club to use to hit the ball carefully into the hole, which is only 108 millimetres (4¼ inches) across.

Players play in turn, a stroke at a time. The player or pair of players who wins one hole has 'the honour' and plays first at the next hole.

You must play the ball where it lies unless there is no possible way of hitting it, when you can lift it and drop it as near to the spot as you can. This adds one stroke to your score as a penalty. If the ball has fallen into water, drop the ball (or another one if necessary) behind the obstacle and try again to hit over it, adding another penalty to your score. This rule applies only to permanent water, which is reckoned to be a hazard. If the ball falls into 'casual water' – a puddle – or on to ground which is being repaired, you can drop your ball in a fresh spot without penalty.

You can play a fresh ball if the one you are using is badly damaged, or you lose it, but you have to add a penalty stroke for a lost ball. If you need to pick up the ball to clean it you must put it back exactly where it was. You are not allowed to smooth out the ground to improve your chances, but if you cut up the turf or scatter sand around when hitting the ball you must repair the damage as well as you can before moving on.

If you break a major rule in match play you lose the hole; if you do so in stroke play you are disqualified.

GYMNASTICS

Gymnastics is a branch of sport in which young people do particularly well, though success means many hours of hard practice. Most of the top women gymnasts are teenagers, and few of the best men are very much older. The sport was founded in the early 1800s by a German school-teacher, Friedrich Jahn. There are six events for men and four for women. Gymnastics forms part of the Olympic Games.

Men's events

Men compete in the following events: floor exercise; pommel horse; rings; long horse vault; parallel bars; and horizontal bar. A team of judges awards points for each event. You have to perform compulsory moves on each apparatus, and also voluntary moves of your own choice when competing at national and international level.

The men's floor exercises are performed on a mat 12 metres (39 feet 6 inches) square. You perform a series of exercises to display your strength and flexibility, including rolls, handsprings, backward and forward jumps, cartwheels and somersaults in the air. The exercises must last not less than 50 seconds and not more than 70 seconds.

The pommel horse is a padded piece of apparatus with two handles (the pommels) on it (see diagram). In this exercise you support your weight entirely on your hands while you swing your legs around the horse, sometimes together, sometimes apart.

The rings are two wooden rings hanging side by side from steel cables 2·55 metres (8 feet 4 inches) above the floor. You leap up and catch hold of the rings, then try to keep them still while you perform various movements, such as handstands and swings. In the cross you bring your arms horizontally on either side while your legs are vertical.

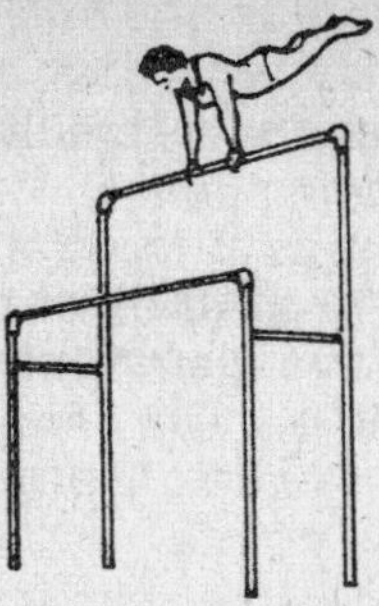

asymmetrical bars

horizontal bar

beam

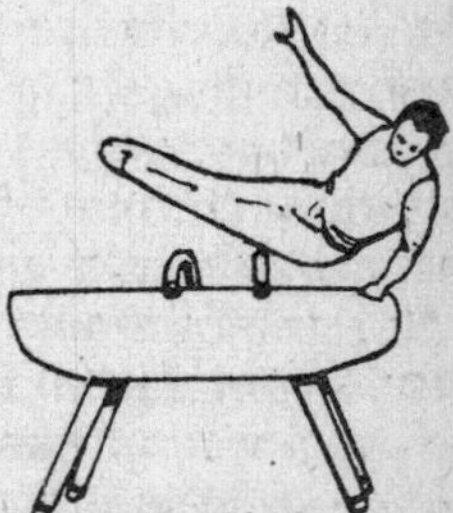

pommel horse

parallel bars

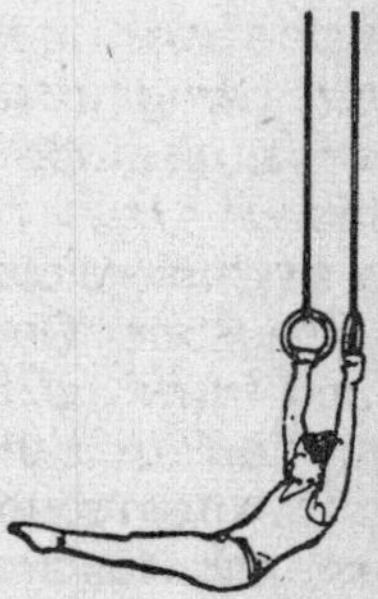

rings

The long horse is similar to the pommel horse but has no handles. You take a run up to one end of the horse, spring up to touch the top with your hands, and land clear the far end. You can somersault, twist in the air or do other movements in flight.

The parallel bars are 1·75 metres (5 feet 9 inches) high. On these you can perform a series of movements, such as handstands and swings, and strength movements, which are done slowly and need great muscle control. You must not touch the ground during the exercise, or you lose points.

The horizontal bar is a flexible bar, placed 2·55 metres (8 feet 4 inches) above the ground. You perform a series of movements, including some that require you to let go of the bar in mid-flight and catch it again.

Women's events

Women compete in the following events: beam; side horse vault; asymmetrical (uneven) parallel bars; and floor exercise.

The beam is a bar 5 metres (16 feet 3 inches) long, and 100 millimetres (4 inches) wide. It is up to 1·2 metres (4 feet) from the floor. In a routine lasting about 1½ minutes you perform turns, running steps, cartwheels, somersaults and other manoeuvres.

The side horse is the same piece of equipment as the men's long horse. You vault across the width of the horse, in much the same way as the men do lengthways.

The asymmetrical bars are at different heights from the floor. One is placed 2·3 metres (7 feet 6 inches) from the floor, and the other 1·5 metres (5 feet). You perform a series of swings, turns and other movements, changing from one bar to another.

Floor exercises are similar to those performed by men. They must last between 1 minute and 1½ minutes, and you perform them to music.

HOCKEY

Hockey is one of the oldest stick-and-ball games, and something very like it was probably played by the ancient Greeks and Romans. The modern form of the game is about 100 years old. Hockey is played on a large pitch, maximum size 91 metres × 55 metres (100×60 yards). The object of the game is to score goals. The team with the most goals wins the game. The goalmouth at each end is made by two upright posts and a crossbar, generally with a net behind to stop the ball. Each team has 11 players. The goalkeeper is allowed to wear protective clothing – gloves, face mask, pads, and heavy boots. The game is played by both men and women.

Each player has a stick with a curved end, flat on the left side. The ball, white and covered with leather, can be struck only with the flat side of the stick. You may stop the ball with your hands when it is in play, but only goalkeepers are allowed to kick it. The game consists of two periods each lasting 35 minutes, with a 5-minute break between them while the teams change ends.

The game is started by two players, one from each team, in the centre of the field, with a bully. Each player taps the ground with his stick, and then taps his opponent's stick. The players do this three times, and are then allowed to hit the ball. A bully restarts the game after a goal.

If you send the ball over the sideline, a member of the opposing team puts it back into play by pushing the ball from a spot on the sideline. Other players must be at least 4·6 metres (5 yards) from the sideline. If the ball goes over the baseline, a defender hits it back into play from not more than 14·5 metres (16 yards) behind the baseline, or an attacker puts it into play from the corner (if the ball was put out by a defender).

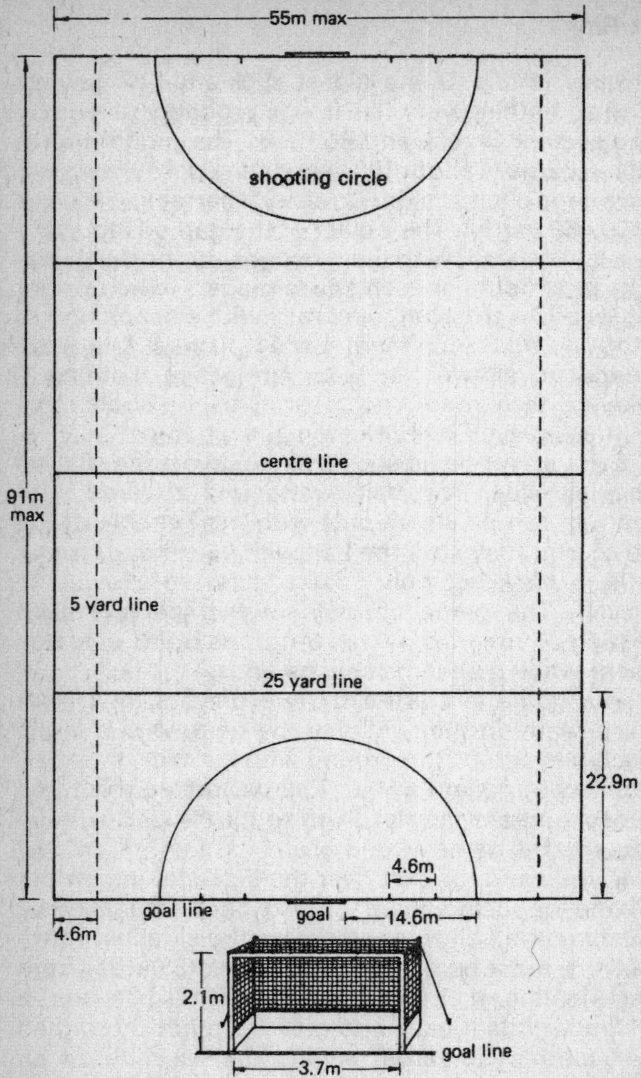

The hockey pitch

HURLING

Hurling is a national game of Ireland, and is a close relative of hockey. It is played on a pitch slightly larger than a soccer pitch: the maximum size is 146 metres by 91 metres (160×100 yards). The object of the game is to score points. The goals have a crossbar and uprights like those of rugby football, but the part of the goal up to crossbar level has a net, like a soccer goal. The game is between two teams of 15 players.

Players use camáns or hurleys, sticks similar to hockey sticks but with wider blades, and a leather-covered sliothar or ball. A ball driven between the goal posts and over the crossbar scores 1 point; a ball driven under the crossbar scores 3 points. The team which scores most points wins.

A game lasts for two halves of 30 minutes each, with an interval up to 10 minutes. The teams change ends at half time.

When the ball is on the ground a player may strike it with the hurley or kick it. When it is in the air he may catch it in his hand, but he must not throw it or carry it by hand. He can, however, throw it with the hurley, or carry it on the hurley's broad blade.

A referee controls the game. He starts it by throwing the ball along the ground between two opposing players, facing each other on the half-way line.

A free puck or stroke is awarded if the ball goes out of play over the end or side lines, or for fouls. Any form of tackling except a shoulder-to-shoulder charge is a foul.

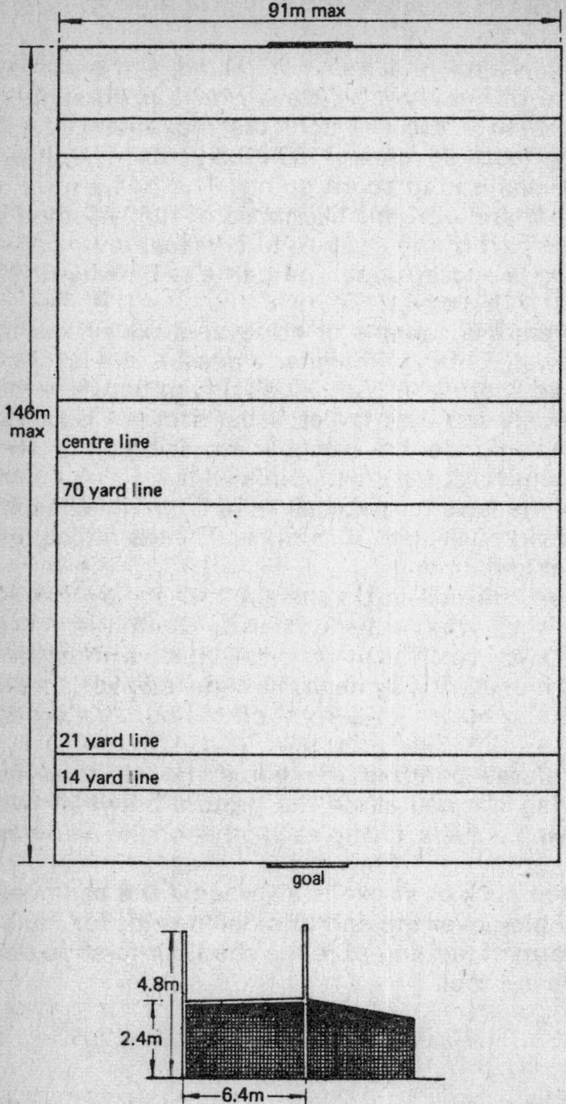

The hurling pitch

ICE HOCKEY

Ice hockey is a fast, skilful game which you are far more likely to see on television than you are to play. It is played only by men. The game is played by two teams of six players, and the object is to score goals.

The pitch is an ice rink, which is marked out by coloured lines under the ice. At each end is a small goal cage, 1·2 metres high by 1·8 metres wide (4×6 feet). The players carry angled sticks similar to those used in ordinary hockey. All players wear some protective clothing – shoulder, elbow and shin pads, and often helmets as well. The goalkeeper also wears a face mask, chest protector and leg pads. All players wear gloves. Instead of a ball there is a puck, a heavy rubber disc which slides over the ice. All the players, and the referees as well, have to be skilled skaters for this game.

Because the game is so fast, frequent substitutions are allowed, and so a complete team consists of up to 20 players. This group includes not more than two goalkeepers, and the captain of each team has two deputies, called alternate captains. Each team has two benches beside the rink. The players not in action wait on one of them. The other is a penalty bench, where players who have infringed the rules are sent for varying periods of suspension.

Each game lasts for three periods of 20 minutes each, with a 10-minute break between them. Play begins with a face-off in the centre of the rink. Two players from opposing teams face each other at the centre spot, and the referee drops the puck on the ice between them. Each then tries to hit it. If play stops for any reason it starts again with a face-off either at the point where play stopped, or at a suitable point close to it.

A goal is scored when an attacking player sends

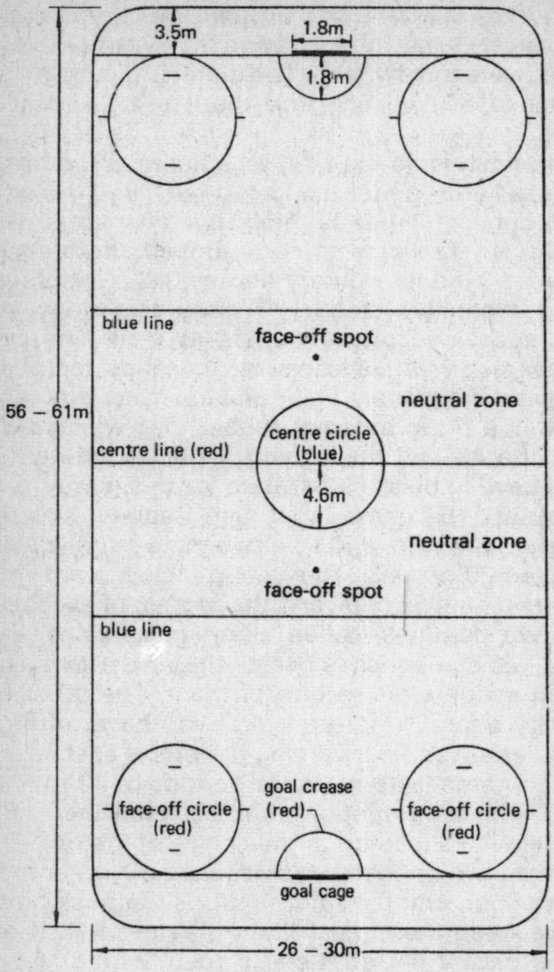

3.5m
1.8m
1.8m
blue line
face-off spot
neutral zone
56 – 61m
centre circle
(blue)
centre line (red)
4.6m
neutral zone
face-off spot
blue line
goal crease
(red)
face-off circle
(red)
face-off circle
(red)
goal cage
26 – 30m

the puck into the goal net. A point is scored for each goal. Other points, called assists, are awarded to the player or players (not more than two) whose play contributed to the goal. The winning team is that which has the most goals.

There is a system of penalties for violation of the rules. A player incurring a minor penalty is suspended from play for two minutes. For a major penalty he is suspended for five minutes; his second major penalty means suspension for the rest of the game, but a substitute is allowed after five minutes. A misconduct penalty is ten minutes' suspension, but a substitute is allowed at once. A match penalty is suspension for the remainder of the game; a substitute is allowed after five minutes. The rule-breaking which results in these penalties includes holding or tripping an opponent, fighting, carrying the stick above shoulder height, swearing, and interfering with the referee or other officials. Icing the puck is also an offence: a player does this if he sends the puck from his team's half of the rink across the opponents' goal-line.

The goal circle shown in the illustration is used in international matches. In National Hockey League matches (Canada and U.S.A.) the marked area at the goal-mouth is rectangular.

ICE SKATING

Skating is a splendid winter hobby in many countries, and with ice-rinks it can be a fine sport all the year round. As far as we know, people have been skating for at least 1200 years. It has been a sport for much less time, and the first ice-rink was built as recently as 1876. If you go skating for fun be very careful where you do it. You are quite safe at a rink, but do beware of frozen ponds. Often the ice looks thick enough, but it can break without warning, and many people have been drowned in this way. The golden rule is only to go where some responsible person has tested the ice and can assure you that it is safe – and then do not go alone.

There are two basic kinds of skating, figure skating and speed skating. You may not be lucky enough to take part in either of these organised forms of the sport, but there are plenty of chances to see them on television, and they form part of the Winter Olympic Games. There are three kinds of competition: solo skating, pairs skating, and ice dancing (which is for a pair of skaters, man and woman). Solo skaters and pairs follow the same sort of programme.

The programme begins with compulsory figures. A skate leaves a tracing as it passes over the ice, and these can be made to form circles and are known as compulsory figures. They begin with the basic figure of eight and become more difficult, with changes of direction in the form of threes, brackets, counters and loops. There are 69 possible combinations, and for each competition a selection of figures is chosen and the competitors are told what they are. Then a quarter of an hour before the start of the competition a smaller number of figures is selected for the actual competition. Women are allowed 4 minutes to skate their compulsory figures,

speed skating

compulsory figures

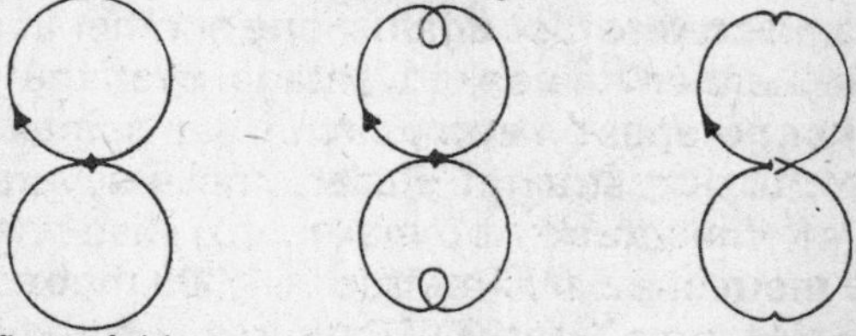

men and pairs 5 minutes.

After the compulsory figures comes the so-called short programme, which lasts about two minutes. Single skaters are required to carry out seven prescribed movements, with the necessary links, and pairs six movements. After that the skater or the pair are free to do their own programme, and for this women are allowed 4 minutes, and men and pairs 5 minutes. The skating is carried out to music, chosen by the competitor. The programme should be varied and must include spins, jumps, spirals and various dance steps. Some of the jumps are named after the skaters who invented them, such as the Lutz and the Salchow. In pairs skating there is an additional move, the lift, in which the man lifts his partner while they are skating.

Ice dancing is similar to ordinary figure skating in that there is a set of compulsory dances, including waltzes, tangoes and quicksteps, followed by a free dance programme of the competitors' own devising. The free part of the dance programme lasts for 4 minutes.

All figure skating and ice dancing is carried out on a rink between 56 and 60 metres long by 26 to 30 metres wide (61–66×28–33 yards).

Speed skating takes place on an oval track. There are two kinds of tracks: the long track has a circuit either 333 metres (364 yards) or 400 metres (437 yards) in length; the short track is about a quarter the length. The standard track has two lanes, and skaters race against one another in pairs. So that neither has an advantage over the other they change lanes on every circuit, at a point known as the crossing straight. Racers make several circuits of the track to make up distances of 10,000 metres, 5,000 metres, 1,500 metres or 500 metres (men), and 3,000 metres, 1,500 metres, 1,000 metres or 500 metres (women). The skater who has the best time for a distance is the winner at that distance. In some competitions each skater competes over all the distances, and the winner is the skater who has the best overall times.

On the short tracks the tracks are wider and up to eight skaters can race against one another. In time events up to four skaters compete in short-distance events, and up to six in longer distances. In elimination races up to eight skaters are allowed, and after every two laps the last skater drops out, until only one is left.

The skates used for speed skating have much longer and thinner blades than those used for figure skating or ice dancing.

JUDO

Judo is a popular combat sport derived from the ancient Japanese system of unarmed combat called jujitsu. It is one of the sports in the Olympic Games. Although children can learn and practice judo from the age of eight, it is a sport that is best learned and carried on under strict supervision, because of the danger of being hurt if you are not properly trained.

The sport consists of various holds and throws, and points are awarded for results from the skill shown in these activities. Competitors wear loose white cotton jackets and trousers, with coloured belts according to their grades. The colour of a belt shows the skill of the contestant: beginners wear white, and experts wear black. The contestants have bare feet.

A judo contest is held generally on a mat 14 metres (46 feet) square with a red danger area 1 metre (3 feet 3 inches) wide around it. A referee controls the fight, and he is helped by two judges who sit at diagonally opposite corners.

A match lasts from 3 to 10 minutes, and a contestant who gains one point wins, but he can also win in other ways. You can score a point by throwing your opponent, or by pinning him to the ground for 30 seconds. Another winning move for seniors is to use a stranglehold to force the opponent to submit, but you are not allowed to use a stranglehold if you are under 16.

Penalty points are counted against you by the judges when deciding on victory, especially in contests where neither contestant scores any points. Severe infringements of the rules mean disqualification. Among the things you must not do are: bend your opponent's fingers back; pick him up off the ground in order to drive him back on to it; fall backwards deliberately on to your opponent when

A typical judo throw

he is attacking from the back; put your hand, arm, leg or foot on your opponent's face; deliberately go outside the contest area.

A kyu (student) goes through nine grades, beginning at 9th and ending at 1st. Different coloured belts indicate the grades, and these colours vary from one country to another, but novices always wear white, the lowest grade is always yellow and the highest is brown. You then become a dan (leader), and are entitled to wear a black belt. There are 12 dan grades. The first six, numbers 1–6, have black belts, the next two have black-and-red belts; and higher grades up to 10th have red belts. No one has yet reached the 11th or 12th grades.

KARATE

Like judo, karate was originally a kind of unarmed combat which developed in Japan. You are more likely to see it on television than to take part in it. The Chinese evolved an earlier form of self-defence called kung fu. Karate is loosely based on kung fu. A karate blow can kill or injure somebody, so for the purposes of sport the contestants 'pull' the blows – that is, they either do not actually hit each other, or touch only lightly. If you do want to practice karate you should do so only in a proper gymnasium and under the supervision of a recognised expert.

A karate contest takes place on a flat surface 8 metres (26 feet) square. The contestants wear white, pyjama-like jackets and trousers, with a belt. The colour of the belt denotes the skill of the contestant. Beginners have white belts, and experts have black ones. Contestants fight in bare feet.

The match is controlled by a referee, assisted by four judges, one at each corner of the fighting area. There are also timekeepers, scorekeepers and other officials. A match lasts from two to three minutes, and ends when one contestant scores two points. The contestants deliver their blows with hands, elbows or feet.

A point is awarded for a technically-good blow or kick that lands correctly, is delivered with good stance and timing, and on the approved target area. Certain areas of the body are not target areas, and contestants must not use some karate techniques which are considered dangerous.

The referee can award penalties for fouls, and most fouls consist of using dangerous techniques, or landing blows heavily. If a foul results in injury to the opponent, the contestant is disqualified.

allowable blows

KARTING

Karting is a form of motor-racing using miniature vehicles, and is the only form of car-sport in which young people can take part. It can be organised by schools and youth clubs, and there is a special category for drivers aged 12 to 16 years. Most karting, however, is an adult sport. The activity originated in the United States, and quickly spread to Europe.

Karts – originally called go-karts – have four wheels, but no bodywork, and the maximum length is 1·8 metres (6 feet). The usual width is 1 metre (39½ inches). Although many karts are capable of high speeds, most races for juniors are run at comparatively low speeds. But because they are so close to the track competitors feel as though they are driving much faster. The karts have steering, accelerator, brakes and gearbox just like full-sized cars, although the karts used by young drivers have no gearboxes.

Racing is over a specified distance, often less than 500 metres (1600 feet). The tracks used vary from purpose-built ones to temporary tracks, but all must have a minimum width of 6 metres (20 feet).

At the start, karts with gearboxes wait on the starting line with their engines running, just as in many ordinary motor-races. For karts without gearboxes, the karts are started, and then cruise round the course to arrive at the starting line together.

Racing is controlled by flag signals from officials at the side of the track. A blue flag warns a driver that he is about to be overtaken. A yellow flag indicates danger, while a red flag means 'Stop at once'. A green flag gives the all-clear. A black-and-white checkered flag indicates that a kart has passed the finishing line.

You must obey the instructions of the officials at

all times. You must also wear the correct clothing for kart racing: a crash helmet with goggles, a heavy leather or PVC suit, stout shoes or boots and gloves. As with many other sports, you should only go karting on proper tracks and under supervision.

A kart and driver

LACROSSE

Lacrosse is a game that originated as a training exercise for North American Indian warriors, particularly those of the Iroquois tribe. The game as we know it now was established in Canada in 1867. It is played between two teams on a grass pitch, and is a kind of stick-and-ball game. The ball is made of hard rubber, while the sticks, known as crosses, have a triangular net at one end which is used to scoop up the ball and throw and catch it. The object of the game is to score goals. The goal posts and their nets are set up at some distance from either end of the pitch, and play can go on behind the goals as well as in front of them.

There are two versions of the game, one for women and one for men. The main differences are in the numbers that make up the teams, the dress they wear, and the size of the pitch.

Women's lacrosse is played between two teams of 12. The ground is the natural size of the field on which it is played, but should be at least 110 metres long by 75 metres wide (120×82 yards). The captains and the umpires decide the boundaries. The only protective clothing you may wear is gloves, except for the goalkeeper who must wear a body pad and leg pads, and may also wear a helmet and face mask. A women's match lasts for two halves of 25 minutes each, with a break of up to 10 minutes between them.

Men's lacrosse is played between two teams of 10. The ground should be a maximum of 100 metres by 64 metres (110×70 yards). Men may wear protective headgear, gloves, arm guards and shin guards, and the goalkeeper may wear thigh pads and body pads as well. They must wear shorts or track-suit trousers. A match lasts for four periods of 20 minutes each. The players change ends after

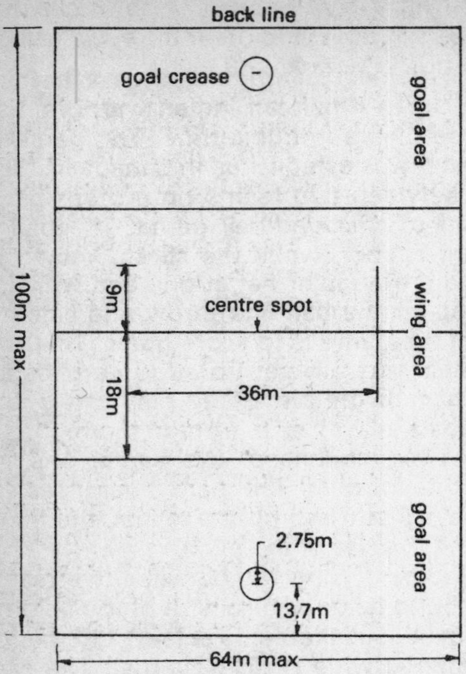

Men's lacrosse pitch

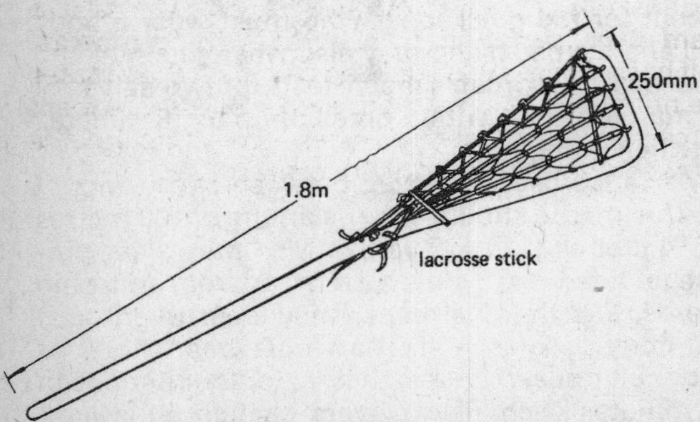

each period. There is an interval of not more than 10 minutes at half time; the other intervals last for no more than one minute.

Play begins for women's teams with a 'draw'. A player from each team stands with her back to her own goal in the middle of the field. The referee, who controls the game, places the ball between the sticks, which are held at waist height. When she calls 'Draw', each player tries to gain control of the ball. Play begins for men with a 'face'; this is similar to a draw, but the players hold their sticks on the ground ready for the whistle.

You can roll or kick the ball along the ground, and carry, throw or catch the ball in your stick. You cannot kick a goal. After each goal play restarts in the centre of the field with a draw or face-off. After other kinds of interruptions play restarts at or close to the point where play stopped. If a ball goes over the agreed boundaries it is thrown in by an opponent of the team whose member last touched the ball. However, if it is a shot at goal or a deflected shot, the ball is thrown in by the player nearest the point at which it goes over the line.

You are not allowed to enter your opponents' goal circle – a circle 5·5 metres (6 yards) around the goal. Men's lacrosse also has an off-side rule: a team must keep at least three men in the opponents' half of the field, and four in its own half. Substitutes are not generally allowed in men's lacrosse, except in certain competitions, when one substitute is allowed. Women can have one substitute.

LAWN TENNIS

The game of lawn tennis gets its name because it was originally played on a grass court. Some grass courts are still in use, though hard courts which can be used in all kinds of weather are now more popular. The game was invented in England in 1874, and was based on an older game, real or royal tennis. The old game is played in an indoor court, and is the game referred to in Shakespeare's play *Henry V*. A few real tennis courts are still in use.

Lawn tennis games are played either as singles (one player against another) or doubles (two against two). Except for fun, men play against men and women against women, though mixed doubles, with each pair containing one man and one woman, are common. The players use rackets to hit a soft ball back and forth over a net. The object of the game is to send the ball into the opponent's court in such a way that the other player cannot return it.

The standard lawn tennis court is 23·77 metres long and 8·23 metres wide (78×27 feet). For doubles a wider court is used, 10·97 metres (36 feet) wide. Either side of the net, and 6·4 metres (21 feet) from it, are the two service lines. See the diagram. The net is 914 millimetres (3 feet) high in the centre. The ball may be white or yellow. Players use rackets with frames made either of wood or metal, and strung with nylon or gut. Before the start of a match, players spin a racket to decide who serves and choice of ends. With a racket, the call is either 'rough' or 'smooth', a reference to the way some of the strings are laced which makes the two faces of the racket look slightly different.

To serve, you stand just behind the baseline (outside the court). For the first service you stand behind the right-hand court, for the second behind the left-hand court, and so on alternately. The same

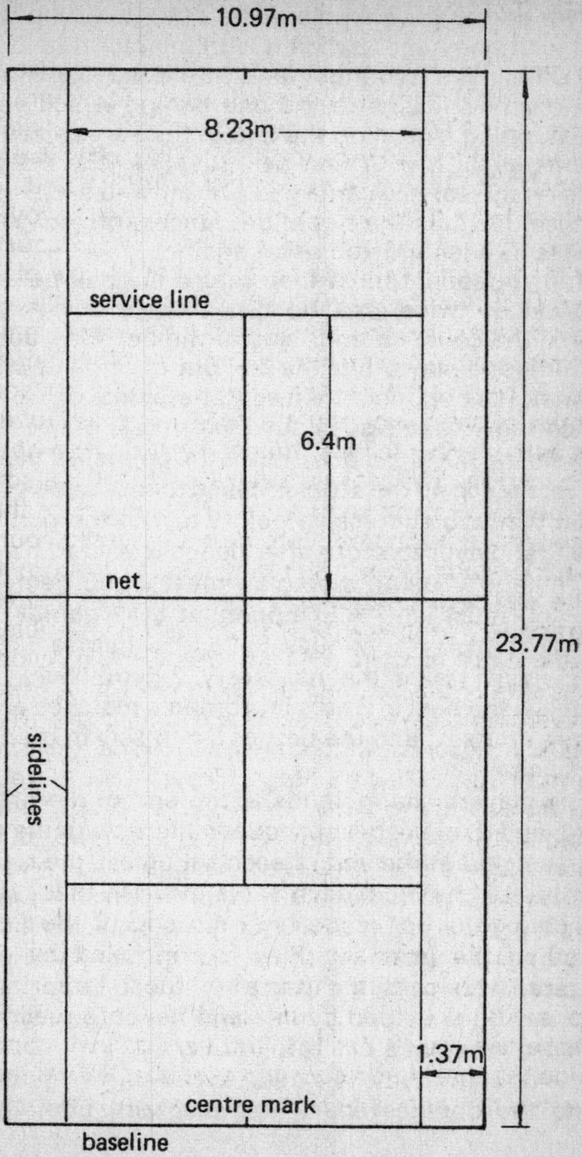
10.97m
8.23m
service line
6.4m
net
23.77m
sidelines
1.37m
centre mark
baseline

player serves for a whole game. You throw up the ball with one hand and hit it with the racket held in the other. The ball must land in the service court diagonally opposite to the one behind which you are standing. A ball on the line of the service court counts as in. If your first ball goes into the net or outside the service court you are allowed a second service. If it hits the net and bounces into court it counts as a let and you serve again.

Your opponent must then return the ball before it bounces twice, and he can place it anywhere within the court on your side of the net. Play goes on until one player hits the ball out of court or into the net. His opponent then scores a point.

Scoring in tennis goes: love (= 0); 15 (1 point); 30 (2 points); 40 (3 points); game (4 points). If both players reach 40 the score is called 'deuce', and you must win two successive points to win the game. The first player to score after deuce is said to have 'advantage'. To win a set you must win 6 games, but you must lead your opponent by 2 games. If necessary, play continues beyond 6 games until one player gains the necessary 2-game lead. A match is the best of 3 sets in women's matches and mixed doubles, and the best of 3 or 5 sets in men's matches.

The players change ends at the end of the first, third, and then every subsequent alternate game of each set and at the end of each set unless the total number of games in each set is even. In that case the change is not made until the end of the first game of the next set. Play is controlled by an umpire, who calls the score. In most important matches he is helped by line and net-cord judges, who call whether a ball is in or out.

The doubles game is similar to the singles game, using the doubles court (see diagram) after the serve. There is a strict order of service in doubles, each player serving for a game in turn.

Because sets between two well-matched players can go on for a very long time, a tie-break can be used when the players reach 6 games or 8 games all. In the tie-break the first player to reach seven points wins the set, provided he has a lead of two points. Play goes on until one player has a two-point lead. The tie-break does not normally operate in the final set of a match. The player whose turn it is to serve is the server for the first point of the tie-break. Then his opponent serves twice, and after that the service alternates, with each player serving twice in succession. The players change ends after every six tie-break points. In doubles, the players serve in rotation in the same way.

Scoring in tennis

Nobody knows for certain how the strange scoring in tennis originated, the four points being counted 15, 30, 40 and game. The most likely origin is that the score was kept at first on a dial like that of a clock, so the scoring would at first have been, 15, 30, 45, 60 (game). The use of 60 disappeared, and 45 became shortened to 40.

The term 'for love', meaning 'for nothing' has been used since the 1600s, and refers to playing a game for the love of it rather than for gain. The term 'deuce' has been used since the 1500s, and derives from the Italian *a due*, meaning 'to two' or 'to both'. All these terms were first used in real tennis, and adopted in lawn tennis.

MOTORCYCLE RACING

For most people motorcycle sports are something to watch either at a meeting or on television. Most of them require special machines and a good deal of skill and practice. However, in some countries there are classes for children, who may ride in special motocross trials, or grass track events long before they are old enough to ride a motorcycle on the public roads.

Competitive motorcycling can be divided into the following major forms: road racing, drag racing, sprints and hill climbs, speedway and ice racing, grasstrack racing, trials and enduro events. Some racing is carried out on near-standard road machines and is called production class road racing. But in most races the motorcycles required to compete successfully in each type of event are highly specialised and purpose-built. All motorcycles must comply with stringent safety regulations. Most races are for solo machines, but there are classes for sidecars in international road racing, and there are sidecar classes in trials, grasstrack and motocross events.

Because motorcycle competitors are very vulnerable if they have an accident, they must all wear protective clothing – a one-piece leather suit, boots, gloves and a crash helmet for road racing.

Road racing is nowadays nearly always carried on over purpose-built circuits, but a very few races are held on public roads closed to other traffic for the duration of the race. The Isle of Man Tourist Trophy (TT) races are an example of this type of event. In road racing the riders make several circuits of the course or carry on racing up to a time limit such as 24 hours (two riders to each machine). The winner is the person with either the fastest time or the greatest number of laps covered, depending on the type of race. Classes are divided by engine size – 50cc, 125cc, 350cc 500cc, 750cc, unlimited – and other restrictions such as weight and the number of cylinders allowed.

Drag racing is a straightforward speed contest. Riders race in pairs over a 400 metre (¼ mile) straight track with a long slowing-down stretch. In most classes special fuels such as nitromethane may be used. So may supercharging and turbo-charging, which are banned in road racing. The winner of each pair is decided on the lowest elapsed time (ET) over the distance, and goes forward to the next round until all but one rider has been eliminated. In sprints (straight track) and hill climb (twisty uphill track) events only one rider at a time is on the course. Each rider completes a number of timed runs, with the fastest time of the day (FTD) winning in each class.

Speedway racing takes place on an oval, 400

drag racing

motocross

road racing

speedway

Different types of machine are required for the various forms of motorcycle racing

metre (440 yard) track surfaced with loose ash and shale. Each race is over a number of laps, usually 4. Riders corner by sliding broadside through the bends and an automatic starting gate is used. Ice racing takes place on a similar oval track covered in hard-packed ice. The machines have long steel spikes fitted to their tyres. Grasstrack machines are similar to speedway bikes, and riders use a similar technique, but the track is laid out in a field and run over grass.

Motocross circuits are specially constructed over a stretch of countryside to include a number of natural and man-made hazards such as streams, steep hills and sudden drops. At international level riders have to complete a large number of laps in this gruelling sport, and they ride machines which are very powerful but also very light, with special suspension systems. Classes are divided by engine size – 125cc, 250cc, 500cc. The winner is the person who completes the distance in the shortest time.

Trials are held over large stretches of countryside which include several sections containing natural hazards such as rock steps, sand, bogs and trees. These test a rider's skill in maintaining balance and machine control, usually at low speed. Observers (judges) at each section award penalty points against a rider who puts a foot down or stops his machine within the section. The winner is the person with the lowest number of penalty points.

Enduro racing and International Six Days Trial events place much more emphasis on speed and accurate timekeeping between checkpoints over large distances on rough ground and ordinary roads. They may include special tests and competitors must keep going without outside help. Enduro machines combine a mixture of motocross and trials motorcycle features. A similar points system to trials scoring is employed to decide the winner.

MOTOR RACING

One of the world's most thrilling sports is motor racing, although it is one you cannot take part in yourself. However, there are plenty of opportunities to watch it at tracks in many parts of the world and on television. Motor racing is almost as old as the motor-car itself, and the first race was held in France in 1894.

There are several classes of motor racing: most of them are held on specially prepared tracks, but some take place on ordinary roads. The main kinds of races are Grand Prix, sports car, stock car and drag races. In addition there are rallies, over long distances, hill climbs and other forms of racing.

There are various kinds of racing tracks. They range from simple ovals with banked curves to longer and more complicated tracks, often with hairpin bends and other features to slow down the drivers' speeds. All circuits used for racing must comply with safety regulations. If public roads are used they must be closed to ordinary traffic.

Cars must conform to standards of construction and design, and are inspected by track officials before each race. In addition, the cars used in various classes must conform to certain engine sizes. All drivers must wear protective fireproof clothing, including a crash helmet.

The cars start lined up on a marked-out grid in several rows. The position each car takes on the starting grid is decided by its performance on practice laps of the course, which are timed by officials. The fastest cars are usually at the front and the slowest at the back. The car with the best practice time is given what is called 'pole position' – that is, one that gives its driver the best advantage on the first corner. Cars may either start from a stationary position, or else they are led around the track in their correct starting order until the leading cars reach the starting line, when the starting flag drops and the race begins.

Flag signals are given as follows: blue, another car close behind; blue (waving), another car trying to overtake; yellow, danger; yellow and red stripes, slippery surface; red, stop; black with a number, the car of that number to stop; black and white chequered flag, the end of the race.

Grand Prix races are those run for what are called Formula 1 cars, which can have engines of up to 3000cc, or half that capacity if they are supercharged. The engines can have up to 12 cylinders. The driver with the best results in Grand Prix races during the year becomes world champion. Less important formulas include Formula 2 where engines are up to 2000cc, and must be based on production engines, that is, those normally manufactured for ordinary use; and Formula 3, where engines are also up to 2000 cc, but must have only 4 cylinders. There are several other formulas, some of them based on engines made by particular manufacturers. The driver who completes the course first wins.

Sports car races are for two-seater cars, including some production cars, but mainly those that are hand-made for racing. The most important sports car races are over long distances, such as the Le Mans 24-hour race held in France every June.

Stock cars are also modified for racing, and many of them are fitted with steel bars to protect the driver if the car should crash and roll over. The rules of stock car racing vary from country to country.

Drag racing is a simple speed contest. Specially-built and tuned cars are timed from a standing start over a distance of 400 metres (¼ mile). The cars race in pairs, and are timed automatically over the distance. A drag-racing track is straight, with a slowing-down stretch of about 800 metres (½ mile). Many drag cars are fitted with parachutes to help them stop.

Rallying is carried out in modified family cars over ordinary roads, parts of which are closed to other cars while the rally passes. Many international rallies are over distances up to 4800 kilometres (3000 miles), and last four or five days, but most events last only one day over a much shorter course. Each car has a crew of two, a driver and a co-driver or navigator. The cars travel over a prescribed route, and are timed at control points. They must report at each control point and have their control books marked. Drivers win points for completing stages inside the allotted time, and lose points for being late or for failing to follow the route. They can also be excluded along the way for having defective lighting or silencers or for driving too quickly on public roads.

Other forms of motor sport include hill climbing, in which competitors have to drive up a twisty hill track in the shortest time possible; autocross, in which competitors race around a track on grass or earth; and rallycross, where the track is a mixture of tarmac and rough ground.

rally car

Formula 1 racing car

NETBALL

Netball is a team game, similar in some ways to basketball. The game was started in England in 1901, and now is played in many countries. It is particularly popular in girls' schools in England.

The game is played by two teams of seven players on a court 30·5 metres long by 15·25 metres wide (100 feet×50 feet). Lines divide the court into three equal areas, two goal thirds and a centre third. A semi-circle around each goal is called the goal circle. The goal is a post 3 metres (10 feet) high with a metal ring on top, over which the ball is thrown. An open net under the ring slows the ball down as it drops through. The ring is just big enough to let a size 5 soccer ball, the ball used, drop through easily. You score goals by sending the ball through the ring. In netball you attack your own goal, not that of your opponents.

Two umpires control the game, helped by a scorer and a timekeeper. A game lasts for four quarters of 15 minutes each, the first and third intervals lasting three minutes and the second 10 minutes. The teams change ends during each interval. Substitutes are allowed only for players taken ill or injured.

The seven players in a team each have specified areas of the court on which they can play, and they incur penalties if they stray into other areas. The playing areas for one team are numbered on the diagram: the numbers read in reverse order for the opposing team. No 5 is the opponents' goal circle; 4 is the opponents' goal third; 3 is the centre third; 2 is the team's goal third; 1 is the team's goal circle. The seven players and their playing positions are as follows: goalkeeper 5 and 4; goal defence 5, 4, 3; wing defence 4, 3; centre 4, 3, 2; wing attack 3, 2; goal attack 3, 2, 1; goal shooter 2, 1. The team

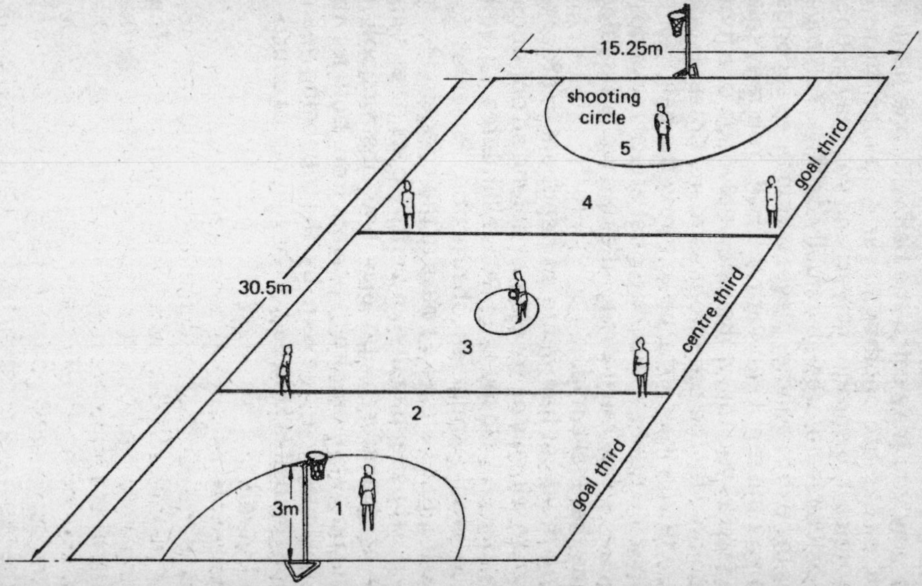

The netball court with one team in position

which starts play is decided by the toss of a coin. Play begins with a pass by the centre, standing in the ring in the middle of the centre third.

In play you may catch the ball with one hand or both, or bat it to another player; you may throw it or bounce it to another player; and you may bounce the ball once before you actually catch it. You must pass the ball to another player within three seconds, and you must not run with the ball. You may take one step as you throw the ball, or pivot on one foot, stepping with the other foot as many times as you like, and you may jump up to throw the ball.

Only the goal shooter and goal attack may score goals, and they must aim for the ring while standing inside the goal circle.

You must not barge into an opponent in order to interfere with his or her play, or defend an opponent with the ball closer than 900 millimetres (3 feet), which would count as obstruction. Penalties for breaking rules are a free pass to the opposing team (the most usual penalty); a penalty pass or penalty shot at goal (for rough play and obstruction); a throw up by the umpire (if players from both teams are involved); a throw-in by the opposing team (when the ball is knocked or thrown out of court).

ORIENTEERING

Orienteering is a modern competitive sport which combines skill in map-reading with the ability to walk or run across rough country. A compass is a useful aid to navigation. You can dress how you like, but arms and legs must be covered. A track suit is a very good choice, with running shoes.

Each competitor is given a map of the course, on which are marked a series of control points. These points are numbered in the order in which you must visit them. The route between the points is not marked, and you have to find your own way to the control points. In some places there are compulsory tracks, and you will find these marked with flags or tape. The map also shows out-of-bounds areas – parts where you must not go.

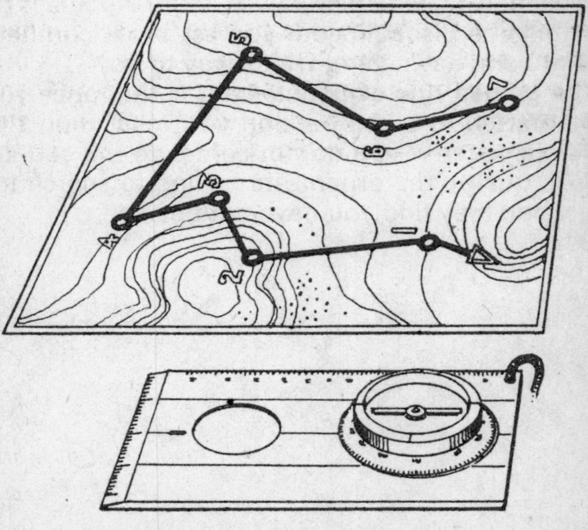

An orienteering map and compass

Competitors start at fixed intervals, so that they cannot follow one another. You have a card which you must stamp at each control point as you get to it. If you stamp the card wrongly you are liable to be disqualified.

There are several kinds of orienteering events. In cross-country orienteering (the main form) you have to go round the series of control points in the shortest possible time. In relay orienteering there is a team, whose members hand over from one to another. Line orienteering is a training exercise in which the complete route is marked on the map for you. In both the relay and line events speed wins the day. In score orienteering each control point has a value of between 5 and 50 points, and you have to amass the greatest possible number of points in a given time. In score orienteering you do not have to visit all the control points, but in the other kinds of orienteering you are liable to be disqualified if you miss out a control point. You may also be disqualified if you ask other competitors or people watching which way to go.

The golden rule of orienteering is that once you have started in a competition you must report to the finish even if you do not complete the course. This is to stop the organisers having to search for you when they find you have not finished.

POOL

Pool is a game similar to billiards and snooker, and it is played on a pocket billiards table. It is especially popular in the United States, and is becoming more popular in Europe.

There are 15 object balls and two cue balls. The object of the game is to strike the object balls with a cue ball so that they go into one of the pockets. The player who first pockets eight balls brings the game to an end.

The 15 object balls each carry a number from 1 to 15, and they are coloured differently for ease of identification. When the game begins they are put into a triangular frame, called the rack, and placed in position as shown in the diagram. The nearest ball (generally the 15) is placed on the foot spot.

The two players start play from behind a line called the head string (see diagram). To decide the order of play, each player sends his cue ball against the cushion at the foot of the table, and the person whose ball comes to rest nearest to the head cushion has the option of starting or not, as he prefers.

The player who starts must either pocket one of the object balls, or cause two balls and his own cue ball to bounce off a cushion. If he fails he loses two points.

In straight pool each player must call the number of the ball he is aiming at, and the pocket into which he intends to send it. If he succeeds he can make a further stroke, and so on until he misses. If he pockets more than one ball he can count them all provided he has pocketed the ball he was aiming at. If not, the balls are brought back into play on the foot spot (or as near to it as possible).

If a player pockets 14 balls in succession, leaving only one ball on the table, the 14 balls are put back into the frame and positioned on the table again. The player then has the option of using the remaining object ball as a cue ball, and pocketing one of the 14 balls from the triangle (which he must name), or of pocketing the last object ball and then sending his cue ball into the triangle in the same shot.

Game is generally 75 or 100 points, and at the end of each game each player's score is added to his total, until the target is reached.

Players lose points if they send their cue balls into a pocket. The player doing so also has a 'scratch' marked against him. The scratch is removed if he pockets a ball successfully on his next turn. If he incurs three scratches in succession he loses 15 points, and must break as if starting the game again.

A player's turn continues from one frame to the next if he has pocketed all 15 balls or pocketed one of the 14 balls in the new triangle.

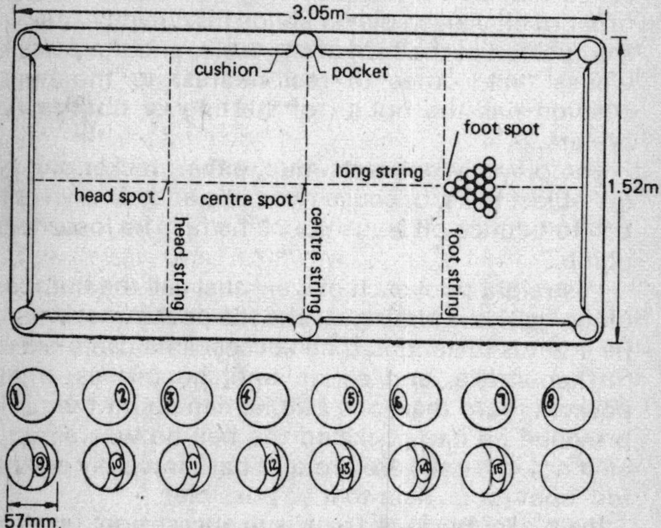

A pool table and balls

ROLLER-SKATING

Probably most of you have a pair of roller-skates, or have used them at some time. Roller-skates were invented sometime around 1760, and have been popular with children (and adults) since about 1850. There are a few simple rules to follow if you are roller-skating for fun: do not use roller-skates on paths beside busy roads; always give way to people on foot; learn how to stop before you venture out with roller-skates; and make sure your skates are in good condition and are firmly attached to your feet.

As an organised sport, there are two forms of roller-skating: artistic skating and speed skating. Artistic skating is divided into three groups: figure skating, free skating, and dancing. All events take place at rinks with wooden or composition floors, usually indoors. In figure skating the skaters carry out 64 different figures or manoeuvres, which they perform on circles painted on the floor of the rink. You have to complete each figure three times. Judges watch for points of style, including having the knees slightly bent; keeping the hands no higher than waist-level; keeping all four wheels on the ground; and maintaining an easy, even flow of movement.

In free skating you have a choice of what movements you perform, to a musical accompaniment. Skaters compete solo or with a partner. A panel of judges awards marks from 1 to 6. In dancing, skaters also perform to music, of their own choice. There are two parts to a dancing competition: a set of compulsory dances, chosen by the organisers of the contest, and a programme of free or own-choice dance movements. As before, judges award points from 1 to 6.

Speed skating is carried out on an oval track, around which the skaters race anti-clockwise. Races

are held over various distances, up to 8 kilometres (5 miles) for men, and 1·6 kilometres (1 mile) for women. Young skaters compete over shorter distances. The winner is the first person to cross the finishing line. Relay races are also held, with each member of the team covering a specified number of laps. In speed skating a skater who is being lapped (overtaken by another competitor) must give way if signalled to do so by an official waving a yellow flag.

A professional form of speed skating popular in some countries is roller derby, in which teams of five men and five women compete. All the men from each team compete in the first part of each race, and then all the women take part. Roller derby is a rough, tough sport in which competitors are allowed to push each other and block their opponents.

ROUNDERS

Rounders is an old English game and is the ancestor of the more sophisticated sport of baseball (see Baseball). Like both cricket and baseball, it is a bat and ball game in which the members of one team bat in turn and try to score runs called rounders while the opposing team fields. The teams, which each have 9 players, then change roles.

The pitch is roughly diamond-shaped. At one corner is the batting square, where the batsman stands, and in the centre, 7·6 metres (25 feet) away, is the bowling square. The batsman uses a stick 46 centimetres (18 inches) long, made of wood or aluminium. The ball is slightly smaller than a cricket ball and not so hard. The batsman's object is to hit the ball far enough to be able to run round the running track (shown on the diagram), touching each of the posts at the other three corners, and finally reaching the fourth post, which is placed to the left of the batting square. If you do this in one go you score a rounder.

You are out if the ball is caught in the air after you hit it; if a fieldsman touches you with the ball; or if a fieldsman touches the post towards which you are running with the ball. But you may wait in safety at posts 1, 2 and 3 until the next ball is bowled, when you can run on round the track. You must always pass outside the posts, and you may not wait at a post where another batsman is already waiting. If you run round the track without hitting the ball you score a half rounder, and if you run round from the first post you also score a half rounder. You do not have to run on unless another batsman is running towards the post you are at.

When bowling, you must deliver the ball underhand, and aim it towards the batsman's batting side, not out of reach and no higher than his head

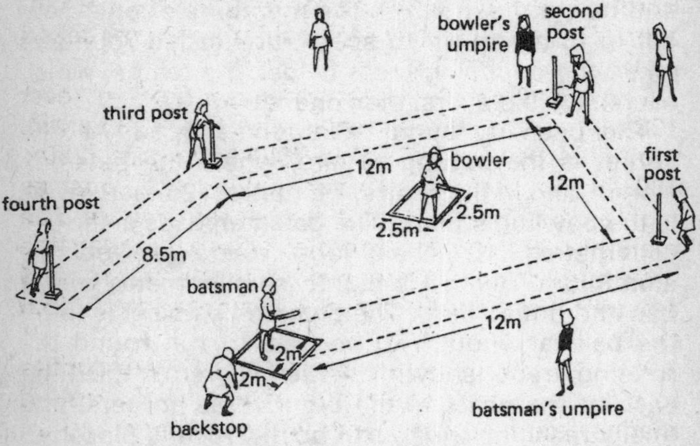

or lower than his knee. The ball must not touch the ground before it reaches the batsman. A ball that fails to meet these requirements is a no-ball. The batsman can ignore a no-ball, or play it if he wishes. But if the bowler delivers a good ball, the batsman must run, even if he fails to hit the ball. The last man in can have the option of three good balls at each turn on the batting square.

If the bowler delivers three consecutive no-balls to the same batsman, the batting team is awarded a penalty half-rounder.

A match consists of two innings for each team, the team to bat first being selected by the spin of a coin. The team with the most rounders wins the match. If the team batting second is ten rounders or more behind at the end of its first innings, the other team may insist that it follows-on – that is, bats again right away.

SHINTY

Shinty is an ancient game from the Highlands of Scotland, and it is something like both hockey and another Gaelic game, the hurling of Ireland (see Hurling). The Gaelic name for the game is camanachd. The object is to score goals, sometimes called hails.

The game is played on a grass field at least 128 metres long by 64 metres wide (140×70 yards), though it can be as big as 230×91 metres (250×100 yards). The goals, called hails, are almost as high as they are wide, and are backed by nets. The markings are few and simple: a semi-circular line around each goal, a small circle in the centre, and a penalty spot a little distance in front of each goal circle.

You play shinty with a caman (club), very similar to a hockey stick, and made of wood. The ball is made of cork covered with woollen fabric and an outer casing of leather, and it is about 50 millimetres (2 inches) in diameter. The game is played between two teams of 12 players each. Two substitutes are allowed, but one of them must be for the goalkeeper, and substitution is permitted only for injury. A referee controls the game, helped by goal judges and linesmen.

A game lasts for two halves of 45 minutes, with an interval of at least five minutes at half time. Play begins with the referee throwing up the ball in the centre of the pitch between two opposing players. Play restarts in the same way and the same place after a goal is scored. After half-time it restarts at the place where it left off.

Unlike hockey, you may use both sides of the stick to hit the ball, and you may hit the ball in the air as well as on the ground. You must not kick the ball or catch it in your hand, though the goalkeeper

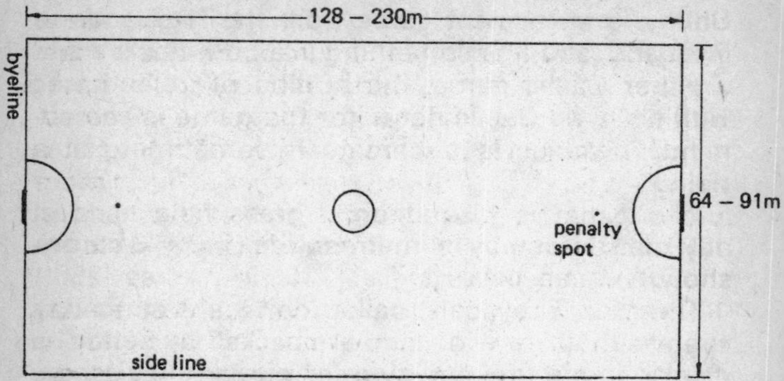

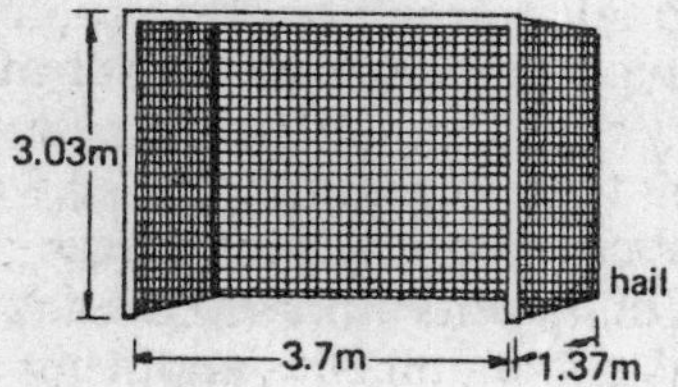

is allowed to stop the ball with his open hand. You must not trip or barge into your opponents, but you may hook an opponent's caman with yours if he is within playing distance of the ball.

If the ball goes off the field it is hit in by a player of the side which did not send the ball out. At the side the ball is hit in from the point where it went out. On the goal line the ball is hit back into play from a point on the pitch anywhere within 9 metres (10 yards) of the goal line. If a defender sends the ball over the goal line the attacking team has a corner hit, taken from one of the two corners on the goal line. If a rule is broken the referee can award a free hit, called a set blow. You are not allowed to stand within 4·5 metres (5 yards) of the player taking the set blow.

SHOW JUMPING AND EVENTING

Until bicycles, motorcars and motorcycles were invented, riding on horseback was one of the main ways of getting about. Today it is a popular sport with children and adults alike. You can learn horsemanship and the elementary rules of riding at a riding school. Some of you may want to learn more and take part in competitions and events, and in any case Olympic and other major riding events are shown on television.

The most advanced competition is the three-day event, a real test of horsemanship. Each day is devoted to a different type of contest: dressage, endurance and show jumping. Dressage and show jumping contests are often held as separate events on their own. In addition, there are one-day and two-day horse trials designed to lead up to the three-day event. A one-day trial consists of dressage, show jumping and a cross country course. A two-day trial is a condensed version of the three-day event.

Dressage tests how well a horse has been trained, and how well the rider knows how to control it. A dressage test is held on a flat, grassy arena, 60 metres by 20 metres (66 yards×22 yards), though a shorter arena, 40 metres (44 yards) long, is used for all novice and elementary tests. You must be riding a registered horse, with a hunting-type saddle and double-bridle, and be correctly and formally dressed. The usual dress for adults is a dark coat, white breeches and top hat. On entering the arena you halt and salute, and then begin the test. A number of routines have been worked out, of varying difficulty, and you are notified in advance of the competition which routine to follow. You must perform the test from memory. It includes moving the horse at a walk, a trot and a canter;

reining back (making the horse move backwards); the piaffer (somewhat like a very slow trot on the spot); pirouettes and half-pirouettes; and smooth, flowing changes from one movement to another. The tests are ridden over a prescribed course, including circles and figures-of-eight.

The endurance test is in four phases, designed to test the stamina and ability of both horse and rider. Phase A consists of riding over roads and tracks at a set average speed – the speed varies with the particular event. Phase B is a steeplechase, over a series of 9–12 obstacles. The obstacles are similar to those used in ordinary steeplechase races. Phase C is similar to Phase A, but over a longer distance. There is then a 10-minute break, during which a veterinary surgeon inspects each horse. Phase D is a cross-country event, over a mixture of rough and smooth ground, during which you and your horse have to negotiate 30–35 fixed obstacles of varying difficulty. Each phase has a fixed time in which it should be completed, and you lose penalty points for any extra time you take. You also lose penalty points if you fall or if the horse refuses to jump an obstacle. If you complete phases B and D in less than the time allowed you are awarded bonus points.

Show Jumping takes place on the last day of a three-day event, and is designed to prove whether a horse is still in good condition after the gruelling riding of the second day. In a three-day event the show-jumping course consists of 10–12 fences or obstacles, none of them higher than 1·2 metres (4 feet), but an ordinary show-jumping event is over a longer course with up to 15 fences. Some of these fences can be 1·7 metres (5 feet 6 inches) high. You must jump the fences in the prescribed order. You are awarded faults (penalty points) for a fall; knocking down an obstacle; a refusal; disobedience by

A horse and rider correctly prepared for dressage tests

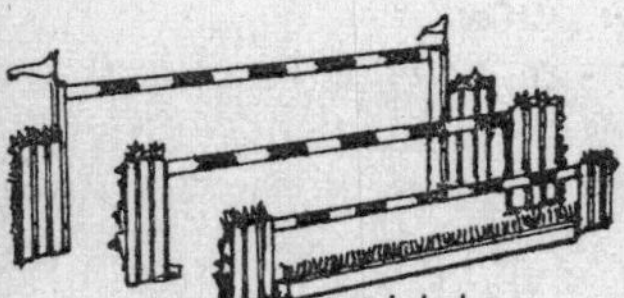

triple bars

double oxer

Typical show-jumping fences

water jump

your horse; or failing to follow the correct route. The winner is the competitor with the fewest faults; if two or more riders tie, then the winner is the competitor who has completed the course in the shortest time. As a rule, the first round is decided entirely on faults, and the final round, called the jump-off, is decided on a faults-plus-time basis. You can be eliminated if your horse is disobedient more than twice, or if you make a mistake in the course and fail to correct it, or if you exceed the time limit.

Endurance riding is a comparatively new sport. In this sport you ride over a long course, generally 160 kilometres (100 miles). The length of the ride and the time taken for it vary from one competition to another. Some competitions allow three days, others only one. The winner is the horse that completes the course in the shortest time and arrives in the best condition. Regular veterinary inspections are held at intervals during the ride, which is over open country for the most part.

Young riders often take part in gymkhanas and mounted games, which may involve picking up obstacles or dismounting to perform certain tasks. The rules of such games vary from one gymkhana to another, but to win you need to have good control over your horse or pony.

SKIING

People have been skiing for at least 4500 years. We know this because a ski that old has been found in a peat bog in Sweden. As a sport, however, it dates from only 120 years ago. There are two basic forms of skiing: non-competitive (skiing for fun) and competitive. Many of you may well have a chance to ski for fun, but competitive skiing is something you are likely to see only on television or perhaps watch while visiting a ski resort.

The rules for skiing as a fun sport are very simple, and they are mostly concerned with safety. Never go skiing unless you are properly dressed and equipped. Make sure that your skis are the right size for you. Your boots must fit firmly and also be comfortable. Be very careful, too, about the bindings, the spring-loaded metal grips which hold your boots on to the skis. These bindings must be adjusted so that your feet come free of the skis if you fall – otherwise you might break your leg. You should always have a strap to link the ski to your boot, or it may run away downhill if it comes off.

The following rules are generally accepted as a code of conduct for all skiers:

Pass to the right of another skier if you cross his path;

If you are uphill from another skier you are responsible for avoiding him; the same rule applies if the other skier is stationary;

If you join a ski-run or trail you should give way to any skiers already on that run;

Do not stop or remain in a spot where you could be a danger to other skiers.

Competitive Skiing

There are six basic forms of competitive skiing, all of which are events in the Winter Olympic

Games. They are downhill, slalom, giant slalom, ski-jumping, cross-country, and biathlon.

In downhill racing competitors must cover a set course in the shortest possible time. The course varies according to the competition. In the Olympics, men must descend a course with a vertical drop of between 800 and 1000 metres (2600–3280 feet), and women ski on a course with a drop of 400–700 metres (1300–2300 feet). The course is marked out by gates – pairs of flags each mounted between two poles. The competitors start at one-minute intervals. People competing in downhill races must wear crash helmets.

A slalom race is run on a downhill course through a series of zig-zags marked out by pairs of flags. The course is designed to test skill in a number of skiing techniques, and contains traverses (skiing across the slope) as well as downhill runs. Each gate consists of two triangular flags, one on each side of the course, and 4–5 metres (13–16 feet) apart. The distance between one gate and the next must not be more than 15 metres (50 feet) or less than 0·75 metre (2 feet 6 inches). Courses for men have between 55 and 75 gates, and those for women between 40 and 60. Competitors race twice, down two different courses. Their times for the two courses are added together, and the competitor with the lowest total time wins. The total vertical drop is much less than for downhill races: 180–220 metres (590–720 feet) for men, 130–180 metres (425–590 feet) for women.

The giant slalom is a cross between downhill and slalom events. The vertical drop is between 250 and 500 metres (820–1640 feet) for men's events, and 250–450 metres (820–1475 feet) for women's races. The course is longer than for the slalom, though not quite as long as for a downhill race, and the gates are further apart than in the slalom. The

21
ski-jumping

slalom course

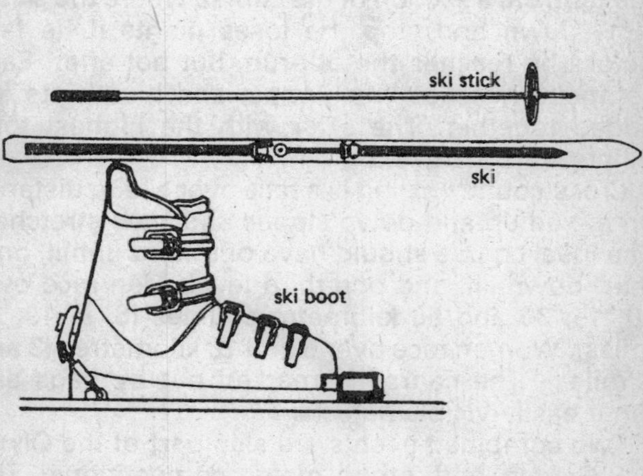
ski stick
ski
ski boot

gates are marked out with the same sort of flags as the downhill course, each supported on two poles, and they are coloured alternately blue and red. Most men's races are over two different courses, but women's events are generally over one course, with one run.

Ski-jumping is the most exciting ski event to watch. Each skier goes down a steep, artificial hill which ends in a sheer drop, the take-off point. The skier then jumps forward and upward, to land on a much gentler slope below. The size of the hill varies according to the competition: for an Olympic event a jump is about 60 metres (66 yards), measured down the slope of the hill from the base of the take-off platform. Competitors are awarded points for the distance they jump, and also for their style. In flight the ski-jumper must keep his skis parallel, close together and his body straight at the hips. He must land with one ski slightly in front of the other, with his knees bent, and his skis should be not more than one ski's width apart. He must then continue to ski forward in an upright position until he reaches the out-run, a section of the course where the skiers slow down and stop. He loses points if he falls before he reaches the out-run, but not after. Each competitor makes two jumps, and his points are added together. The skier with the highest total points wins the event.

Cross-country skiing is a race over a long distance on mixed up-and-down slopes and level stretches. The ideal course should have one-third uphill, one-third downhill, and one-third level. Men race over 10, 15, 30 and 50 kilometre courses (6, 9, 19, 31 miles). Women race over 5 and 10 kilometres (3 and 6 miles). The course is marked out by flags and other easily-visible objects.

Two combined events are also part of the Olympic Games and other major competitions. The

Alpine combined event consists of three races – downhill, slalom and giant slalom – in which all competitors take part. The winner is the person with the best total number of points for the three events. The Nordic combined is a mixture of ski-jumping and cross-country, and as in the Alpine combined the winner is the competitor who scores the highest total of points for both events.

The biathlon event is also a combined one, and unites cross-country skiing with ·22 rifle shooting. Each competitor sets off on the cross-country course carrying his unloaded rifle and ammunition. At fixed points during the course he fires at each of five targets, some of the firing events being from a standing position, and some lying down. If he misses he receives a time penalty. Competitors in relay events have to complete a penalty loop of about 50 metres (55 yards) for each miss.

Between the firing events competitors must ski for at least 3 kilometres (1·8 miles). The Olympic and World Championship races are 20 kilometres (12·4 miles), four shoots; 10 kilometres (6·2 miles) sprint, two shoots; and 4×7·5 kilometres (4·7 miles) relay.

SKITTLES

Skittles is an old name for an even older game. It was played by Egyptian children 7000 years ago. The object of the game is to knock over a number of skittles or pins by bowling or throwing a ball or other object at them. Two other modern versions of the game are ninepins and tenpin bowling.

Skittles is the oldest form of the game and is still popular in European countries. The number of pins used varies, but four is a popular number. The pins or skittles are arranged in a diamond pattern at one end of an alley or run, which should be 6·4 metres (21 feet) long. To play you stand at the opposite end of the alley to the skittles and hurl at them a cheese, a thick flat disk of hard wood which weighs about 4·5 kilograms (10 pounds).

Ninepins is very similar to skittles. Nine skittles or pins are arranged in the diamond pattern. Though a cheese may be used, most players use a hard wooden ball about 125 millimetres (5 inches) across. You have three throws, and score 1 point for each skittle you knock over. The pins are set up again between throws. In a match the player with the highest number of points wins.

Tenpin bowling is the American version of the game. The people of the United States used to play ninepins, but they gambled so much that ninepins was made illegal in the mid-1800s. So they added an extra pin and created tenpins. Actually, tenpin bowling had already been played in England some 60 years earlier. The pins used in modern tenpin bowling are bigger than the traditional skittles. The balls are hard and heavy, and made of rubber or plastic. A ball is 216 millimetres (8½ inches) in diameter, and weighs up to 7·25 kilograms (16 pounds). The bowling lane is just over 19 metres (62 feet) long. Just beyond one end of the lane the

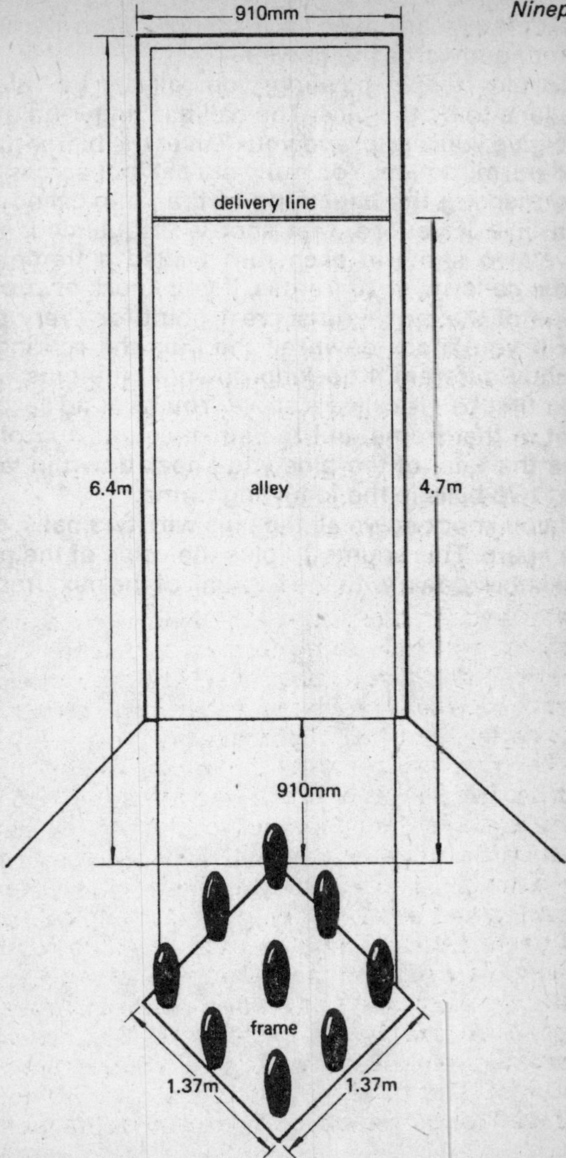
910mm
delivery line
6.4m
alley
4.7m
910mm
frame
1.37m
1.37m

ten pins are arranged in a triangle, with its apex pointing towards the bowler.

To play tenpin bowling, you roll the ball along the lane to hit the pins. The ball has finger-holes in it to give you a grip, and you deliver the ball with an underarm motion. You must not set foot across the line marking the beginning of the lane, called the foul line. If you do, that shot is disqualified. You have two shots in each turn (called a frame). A game consists of 10 frames. If you knock over only some of the pins, you score 1 point for every pin. But if you knock down all the pins the scoring is slightly different. Knocking down all the pins with your first ball is called a strike. You have no second shot in that frame, but the strike counts 10 points plus the total of the pins you knock down in your next two balls in the following frame.

If you knock down all the pins with two balls, this is a spare. This counts 10 plus the value of the pins you knock down with the first ball of the next frame.

SNOOKER

Snooker is a game related to billiards, and it is played on a standard billiards table with pockets. Players use 21 object balls and a white cue ball. Points are scored by potting balls – that is, hitting them with the cue ball so that they go into pockets. The game is normally played by two people, but it may be played by pairs or teams. The player or partnership with the most points wins.

There are 15 red balls, worth one point each, and six 'colours', whose values are as follows: yellow 2 points; green 3 points; brown 4 points; blue 5 points; pink 6 points; black 7 points. At the start of play the balls are positioned as shown on the diagram, each of the colours sitting on a spot. The reds are positioned by putting them into a triangular frame, which is then lifted off, and a game is often known as a 'frame'. The players toss a coin to decide who starts the first game, and after that they take it in turns. The player who starts plays the cue ball from the 'D' at the foot of the table. He is said to 'break', because he breaks up the triangle of red balls. But the word 'break' is also used for the total score a player makes in any turn.

When you are playing, you must pot a red before you pot a colour. The red stays down, but the colour is replaced on its spot. Your break lasts until you fail to pot a ball. You can pot any red, even by accident, but you must always say which colour you are aiming for. If you miss the colour penalty points are awarded to your opponent – the value of the colour for the three highest colours, and 4 for the three lowest. If you aim for one colour and hit another, you forfeit whichever score is the higher, that of the ball you missed or that of the ball you hit. You also lose 4 points if you hit the cue ball into a pocket, or miss a red.

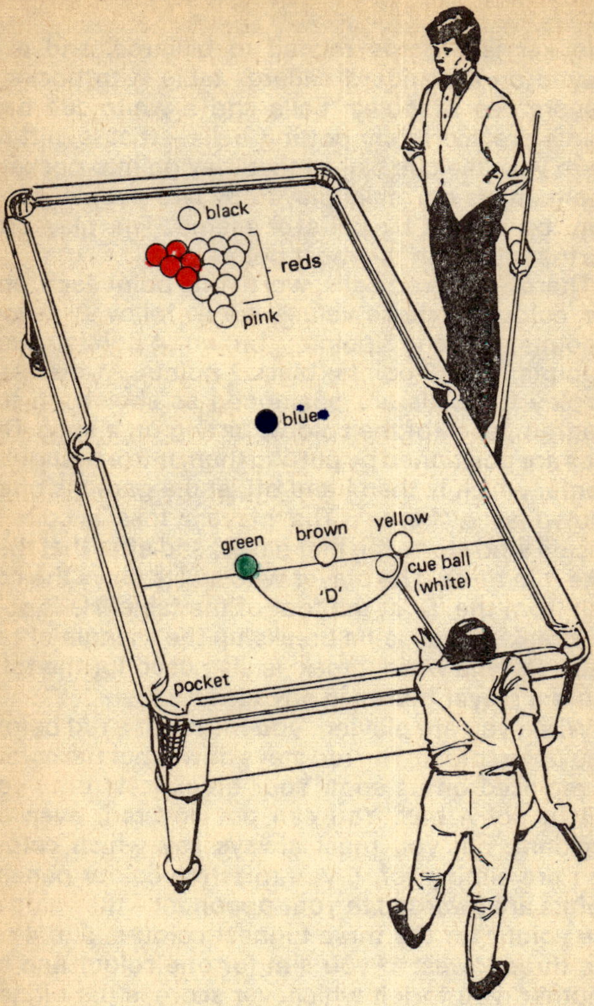

Starting a game of snooker

You may aim for any colour you wish. When a player pots the last red he tries for a colour, and if he pots it that ball comes back into play for the last time. The colours must then be potted in ascending order of value, beginning with the yellow. If the players end with equal scores, the black is brought back and the players take turns to try to pot it, with the cue ball in the D where play began. Incidentally, if the white ball goes down it is brought back into the D to restart play, and the player who put it down loses 4 penalty points.

A player is said to be snookered if he cannot aim directly at the ball he is due to hit next. However, if you are snookered because your opponent has made a foul stroke – that is, incurred a penalty – you may play any ball you wish, and it is treated as scoring the value of the ball you should have hit.

The cues are identical to those used in billiards, and so are the rests.

SQUASH RACKETS

The game of squash rackets was founded on an earlier game called just 'rackets'. It was probably invented at Harrow School in England about 130 years ago. The game is similar to lawn tennis, and is played by two players with rackets and a small rubber ball.

The difference between squash and lawn tennis is that there is a wall where the net would be in tennis. Both players are in the same play area, taking it in turns to hit the ball against the wall. They must hit it above the 'tin', a strip of metal along the foot of the wall, which makes a loud noise when the ball strikes it. The ball must also be below the out-of-court line, near the top of the wall. Balls above this line are out of court. The line extends downwards along the side walls of the court, which are also used in play (see diagram for the marking of the court).

In play, one player serves, and the two then take it in turns to hit the ball until one player fails to return it before it bounces twice on the floor, or fails to strike the front wall above the tin, or hits the ball out of court. The server is known as hand-in, and his opponent as hand-out. If hand-in wins the rally, he scores a point. If hand-out wins it, he takes over the service. A game is won by the player who first reaches 9 points, and a match is the best of 5 games. If the score in a game reaches 8-all, hand-out chooses either 'no set', and the game continues until it is won 9–8, or 'set two', in which case it continues to 10–8 or 10–9.

You serve from one of the two service boxes shown on the diagram. You must have at least one foot within the box at the moment you hit the ball. You must hit the ball directly on to the front wall, below the out-of-court line but above the cut or

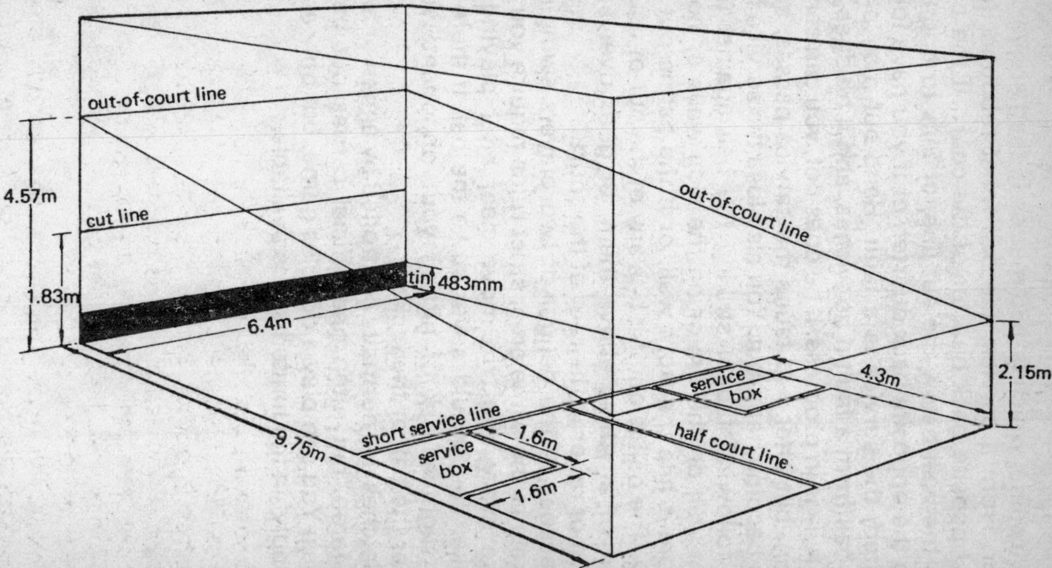

A squash court

service line, which is 1·83 metres (6 feet) above the floor. From a service, the ball must rebound into the opposite back quarter of the court. If the ball hits the wall below the cut line, or fails to bounce into the opposite back quarter, or if you have foot-faulted, the service is a fault. Hand-out may play the ball from a fault if he wishes, and if he does so the rally is in progress. If he does not, you can serve again, but after two faults the service passes, and you become hand-out. You also lose the service for the following faults: striking the ball against the front wall on the tin, or on the side walls or floor before it hits the front wall, or if the ball is out of play. The ball is out if it hits any of the out-of-court lines, or anything above them, or goes over any beam or rafter in the roof of the court.

Because of the danger of two players swinging rackets in the same area, strict rules require you to make every effort to move clear after playing a stroke. You should never strike the ball if there is the slightest risk of hitting your opponent with either the ball or the racket.

Matches are normally controlled by a marker and a referee, but often one official carries out both duties. You can play a doubles game, but only as a 'friendly' in the limited space available.

TABLE TENNIS

Table tennis was invented in the late nineteenth century as an indoor form of lawn tennis. It was at one time known as Ping-Pong, a name invented and patented by a company which made table tennis equipment. Either singles or doubles can be played, as in lawn tennis, but the singles game is the more popular.

A full-sized table tennis table is 2·74 metres long by 1·52 metres wide (9×5 feet). It is 760 millimetres (2 feet 6 inches) high. It is perfectly possible to play on a smaller table for fun, provided the proportions of width and length are the same as a full-sized table. The net is 153 millimetres (6 inches) high. The ball is very light, made of celluloid or other plastics. The rackets, also called bats or paddles, may be any size, shape or weight, but must have a thin wooden blade. The blade is generally covered with rubber to give a better grip on the ball.

Game is 21 points. You score points if your opponent fails to make a good service or a good return, or strikes the ball out of turn in a doubles match. You serve by holding the ball on the palm of one hand, flipping it up and hitting it with the bat. The ball must strike the table your side of the net and then bounce over to strike the table on the opponent's side. A good return is made when you strike the ball, after it has bounced your side, so that it clears the net and strikes the table on the other side. You must not volley – that is, strike the ball before it hits the table. The ball is allowed to touch the net on returns, but not on a serve. If the ball touches the net when you are serving a let is called, and you serve again. No points are scored from a let.

Players toss a coin to decide who shall serve first. You change service after every five points are

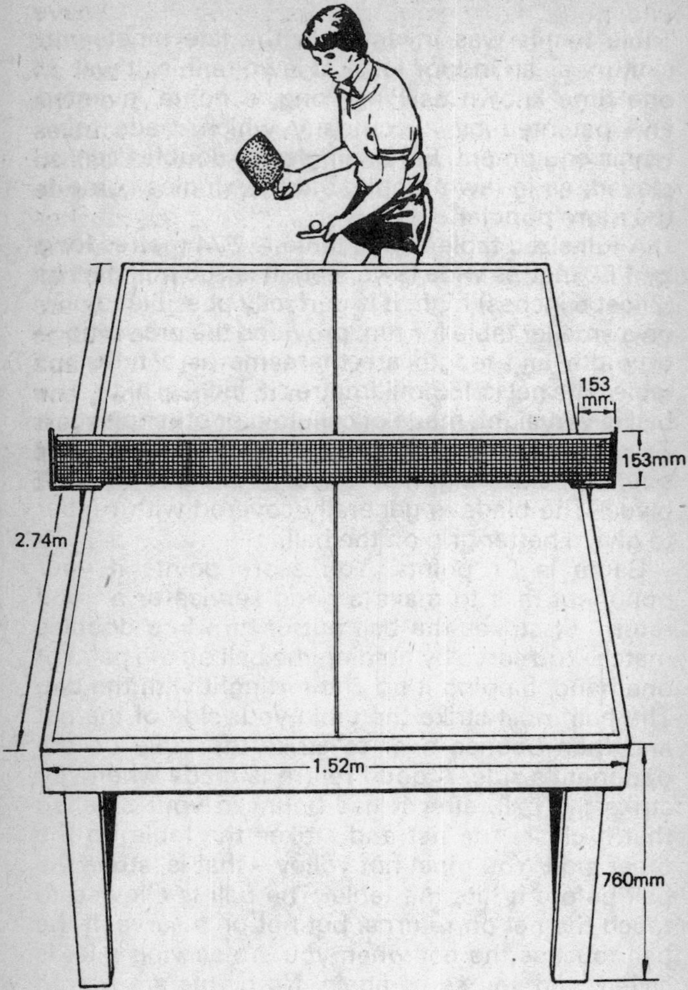
153
mm.
153mm
2.74m
1.52m
760mm

scored, unless you reach 20–all. Then service changes at every point. The first player then to have a lead of 2 points over his opponent wins the game.

When serving in singles you may hit the ball on to the table anywhere, as long as it lands on the correct side of the net, but the rules for doubles play are different. In doubles, you strike the ball so that it first touches the right half-court on your side of the net, and then passes over the net and touches the court diagonally opposite – that is, the receiving player's right-hand court. Partners must hit the ball alternately when making returns. If A and B are partners against C and D, A serves to C, who returns it to B, who returns it to D, who returns it to A, and so on. The service changes in the same way, and you always serve from a right-hand court. Players or pairs change ends after each game. A match is a single game, the best of 3 games, or the best of 5 games.

VOLLEYBALL

Volleyball was invented in the United States in 1895 and is now popular all over the world. It is one of the sports in the Olympic Games. Two teams of players face each other on a court and punt a ball back and forth over a high net. The object of the game is to prevent the ball touching the ground on your side of the net.

The court is 18 metres long and 9 metres wide (60×30 feet). The net is suspended across the centre so that its top is 2·44 metres (8 feet) from the ground for men, and 2·24 metres (7 feet 4 inches) for women. The ball is similar to a football, inflated with a leather case, but slightly smaller and much lighter. Each team has six players, with up to six substitutes. A referee controls the game, helped by an umpire and two or four linesmen. A match is the best of five sets. The right to serve first is decided by tossing a coin. Only the serving team can score.

At the beginning of the game the players line up in two rows of three, as shown on the diagram. Once the ball is served they can go anywhere they like on their side of the net, but only the front row may play attacking shots. But they must take up their correct positions for the next serve. The serve is made by the player on the right hand in the back line, and he stands behind the baseline to serve. He continues to serve until the team commits a fault, when the service passes to the other team. The members of the team that take the serve change position, moving clockwise one place. In this way, every member of the team has a chance to serve.

You can play the ball with any part of your body above the waist, but you must not hold it. However, it is usual to play the ball with the hands or forearms. When serving, you must strike the ball with your open hand, fist or arm. You and your

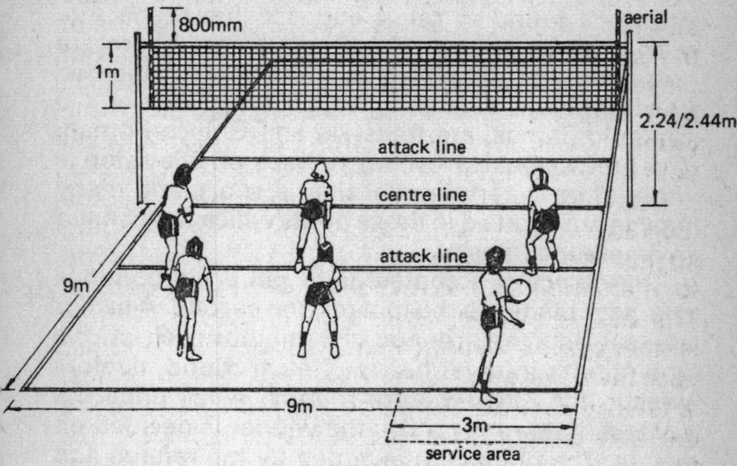

team mates may touch the ball up to three times before sending it over the net. In this way, you can pass it from one to another to gain the best attacking position.

The ball may touch the net during play, though not during service; you must not touch the net or aerials yourself. Neither may you reach over the net to touch the ball, except when defending your opponents' attack.

The main faults, which end a team's serve, are as follows: if the ball touches the ground on the serving side; if a player touches the ball twice in succession; if more than three players touch the ball; if the ball goes out of court; if the ball goes round the end of the net; or if the ball touches a player below the waist.

Each team can have two 30-second time-outs during a set.

WRESTLING

Wrestling is one of the oldest of all sports, and drawings found in caves suggest that Stone Age men used to wrestle 20,000 years ago. There are about 50 different styles of wrestling, but the two used by most amateurs, which form part of the Olympic Games, are freestyle and Graeco-Roman. The professional wrestling you see on television is more of an entertainment than a sport, and many moves are allowed in those bouts which are banned in amateur contests.

The object of a contest is to pin an opponent's shoulder blades to the mat for one second. A senior contest lasts for 3 rounds of 3 minutes each, with a one-minute interval between each round. Juniors wrestle for 2 two-minute rounds. A fall ends the contest. If there is no fall, the winner is decided on points. The points are awarded by the referee and judge, who controls the contest, and two judges.

Points are awarded as follows: 1 point for bringing your opponent down, moving from underneath to above and gaining control, and if your opponent receives a caution; 2 points for holding your opponent in danger of a fall for less than 5 seconds; 3 points for holding him for 5 seconds. For international competitions the result of each bout is converted into penalty points – for example, 0 penalty point for winning by a fall, 3 penalty points for losing by a fall, 4 penalty points for losing by 12 or more points. Contestants who receive more than 6 penalty points are eliminated, and bouts continue until 3 contestants are left in, and they are ranked first, second and third (or, at the Olympics, gold, silver and bronze medal-winners).

Wrestling takes place on a padded mat (not in a ring like professional wrestling). The mat is 12 metres (40 feet) square and the wrestling area is 9 metres

Graeco-Roman

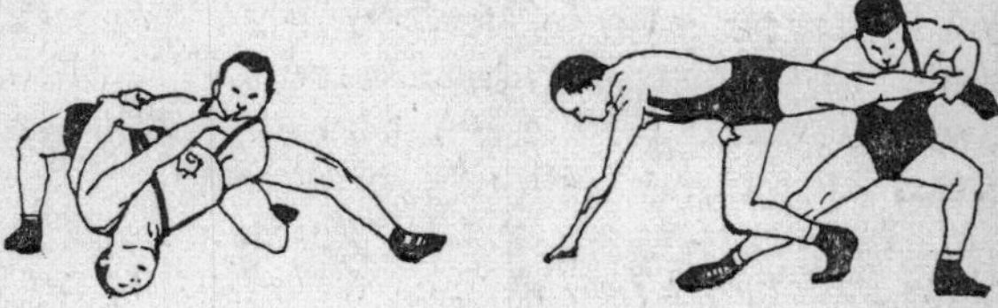

freestyle

Typical Graeco-Roman and freestyle wrestling holds

(30 feet) in diameter. A smaller mat is used for some amateur contests, particularly for juniors. The contestants wear leotards (one-piece garments) in red or blue, and special boots. They must not cover their skin with oil or grease, which would make it difficult for an opponent to hold them.

The rules list moves and holds which are not allowed. Basically, any hold or move which is potentially dangerous is forbidden, and so are back-hammers (forcing an opponent's arm behind his back), stepping on his feet, touching his face between the eyebrows and the mouth, or going off the edge of the mat. If either wrestler goes off the mat the contest is halted and starts again in the middle of the mat. Other infringements lead to a caution. Three cautions mean disqualification. These rules apply both to freestyle and Graeco-Roman wrestling. In addition, in Graeco-Roman wrestling you must not use your legs to trip or grip your opponent, nor may you hold him below the waist.

SAFETY IN SPORT

Accidents do happen in sport and people can be hurt, sometimes badly. But nearly all accidents can be avoided if you take a few very simple precautions.

The first precaution is to follow the rules of whatever sport you are engaged in very carefully. You will enjoy the game more and play it better if you do – and remember that in a team game players who allow themselves to be injured through carelessness are letting their team-mates down.

Always use the proper equipment, and make sure that it is in good order. If the rules specify protective clothing, wear it. It is not clever to do without. Make sure you understand exactly what you ought to be doing. If you are using apparatus, be sure that someone who really knows has shown you how to use it. You should never engage in some sports, such as judo, without an instructor or someone responsible present to make sure that you come to no harm.

Keep your temper. A great many accidents happen because a player loses his temper and does something silly or careless. Remember, too, that unless you stay calm you cannot concentrate properly on what you are doing – so you will not do so well.

Many sports require you to be really fit. If you are not fit, do not be afraid to say so. If you are hurt in any way while taking part in any sport, report the injury at once – it may not stop you carrying on, but in some cases playing on will only make matters worse.

Another source of trouble is litter. Make sure that the area in which you are playing is free of any obstructions, and out of doors be particularly careful to clear away any sticks, bits of metal or glass, and other rubbish.

Remember that the need for safety precautions does not end when you finish your game. Many people are hurt by carelessness in changing-rooms and showers – it is very easy to slip on a wet floor, for instance.

Finally, it is a good idea to have some knowledge of first aid, and to know where the first-aid kit is kept.

All these hints will help you to get more fun out of your sport, not less.

More Beaver Books

We hope you have enjoyed this Beaver Book. Here are some of the other titles:

Famous Lives: Sport A Beaver original. Football players, mountaineers, land speed record breakers, swimmers, motorcycle racers, this book is packed with fascinating information about 176 of the world's greatest sporting personalities. Devised by James Moore, written by Eric Inglefield and illustrated by Peter Dennis.

Danger Girls A Beaver original. Sixteen thrilling, real-life tales in which girls find themselves – often all alone – in some amazingly dangerous situations. Meet a fearless spy from the American Civil War, another from the Second World War, the girl who became a highwayman and even a female pirate or two! Written by Robin May and illustrated by Trevor Parkin

These and many other Beavers are available at your local bookshop or newsagent, or can be ordered direct from: Hamlyn Paperback Cash Sales, PO Box 11, Falmouth, Cornwall TR10 9EN. Send a cheque or postal order, made payable to The Hamlyn Publishing Group, for the price of the book plus postage at the following rates:

UK: 30p for the first book, 15p for the second book plus 12p a copy for each extra book ordered to a maximum of £1·29;
BFPO and EIRE: 30p for the first book, 15p for the second book plus 12p a copy for the next 7 books and thereafter 6p a book;
OVERSEAS: 50p for the first book and 15p for each extra book.

New Beavers are published every month and if you would like the *Beaver Bulletin*, which gives a complete list of books and prices, including new titles, send a large stamped addressed envelope to:

Beaver Bulletin
Hamlyn Paperbacks
Banda House
Cambridge Grove
Hammersmith
London W6 0LA

383695